**How the Bureaucracy
Makes Foreign Policy**

How the Bureaucracy Makes Foreign Policy

An Exchange Analysis

David Howard Davis
Rutgers University

Lexington Books
D.C. Heath and Company
Lexington, Massachusetts
Toronto   London

To My Mother and Father

Table of Contents

List of Figures

List of Abbreviations

BLS	Bureau of Labor Statistics
DISC	Domestic-International Sales Corporation
DOLITAC	Department of Labor International Technical Assistance Corps
ELDO	European Launch Development Organization
ERS	Earth Resources Survey
ESRO	European Space Research Organization
Foggy Bottom	State Department Headquarters
FSO	Foreign Service Officer
FSR	Foreign Service Reserve Officer
GATT	General Agreement on Tariffs and Trade
ILAB	International Labor Affairs Bureau
NAC	National Advisory Council on International Monetary and Financial Policies
OMB	Office of Management and Budget
PAS	Participating Agency Staff
PASA	Participating Agency Service Agreement
PL 480	Public Law 480: Agricultural Trade Development and Assistance Act of 1954
SDR	Special Drawing Rights
16th Street	AFL-CIO Headquarters
STR	Special Trade Representative

Foreword

This book draws our attention to a process that has become increasingly important in the American political system—the interaction among executive agencies charged with responsibility for carrying on government programs. Professor Davis focuses on the exchange of goods and services among the State Department and three other executive agencies—the Treasury, NASA, and the Department of Labor. His study illuminates our understanding of the way in which such interorganizational arrangements affect the development of public policy.

Looking at executive organizations in terms of the lateral ties that bind them together is quite unusual in studies of government bureaucracy in the United States. More commonly, our perspective is a hierarchical one. We concern ourselves with the lines of authority that run up and down in the executive branch between the White House and the executive departments, departments and their subordinate bureaus, or headquarters and the field. The distribution of authority between superior and subordinate officials dominates our analysis of organizational decision and activity.

A similar preoccupation with hierarchy is visible in virtually all proposals for administrative reform in the United States. Recommendations for executive reorganization commonly stress the need to center authority in the heads of agencies—by moving authority upwards from bureaus to departments, or by strengthening the capacity of headquarters to monitor decisions at lower levels. The common remedy proposed for the ills of metropolitan areas is to replace the present multiplicity of governmental units with a single authority having jurisdiction over all or a major part of the public functions performed in the region.

The drift of change in American government and society has also been toward hierarchy—witness, for example, the familiar migration of power from local to state and from state to national units of government. Political scientists in the United States have generally supported such change. Indeed, when they serve on study commissions and other reform institutions, specialists in public administration generally sponsor it. Such a predisposition toward hierarchy is visible in efforts to reform political as well as bureaucratic institutions. Academic proposals for the renovation of Congress or of American political parties usually stress the need to bolster the leadership of such institutions.

It is not surprising, therefore, that Professor Davis draws his models for the study of interorganizational exchange not from the traditional literature of political science but from economics, since this discipline studies organizations that cooperate in the private arena not by virtue of commands from above but because they perceive joint interests in doing so. Such interests stem primarily from the possibility of exchanging services or commodities in mutually advantageous ways. In a strikingly innovative analysis, Professor Davis applies not only the notion of exchange but a variety of other concepts derived from economic analysis to the study of public agencies, including price, utility, and investment. The incentives that shape the behavior of these organizations toward each other are shown to be not altogether different from those that condition the activity of private firms linked together in a market system.

The fact that this study focuses on the horizontal rather than the vertical ties that bind organizations together is by no means its only innovative characteristic. It also breaks new ground by showing how frequently the interests of public agencies complement rather than conflict with each other. The few studies we have of interaction among public agencies tend to emphasize the adversary character of such relationships—the way these organizations compete for the resources necessary for survival, including statutory authority, legislative appropriations, or public favor. This is a common theme in studies of the relations among executive agencies in such fields as conservation and national security administration, where agencies are often shown engaged in a zero-sum struggle for power in which gains for one must be offset by losses for another.

Professor Davis directs our attention instead to the fact that executive agencies often assist each other in achieving their goals. The State Department's use of NASA astronauts on goodwill trips abroad helps it attain one of its primary goals—the promotion of good relations between the United States and the countries visited. By assigning Foreign Service officers as labor attachés the State Department gains an acceptance from the labor movement abroad that its own diplomatic professionals could never attain. Its linkage with Treasury provides the department with an economic expertise that is in short supply within its own organizational boundaries.

Thus, at one level the exchange model presented in this study is a powerful explanatory tool—clarifying the origin and effects of the bilateral and multilateral arrangements that coordinate the activities of executive agencies in the foreign policy arena. The family of organizations that conducts American policy abroad is shown to be not altogether polarized by sibling rivalry. Agencies do assist one another when it is in their interest to do so, and their interests are served in this fashion more often than has traditionally been recognized. From this perspective, Professor Davis has made a highly original contribution to our understanding of organizational behavior and decision-making in public bureaucracy.

But at another level this study is of considerable practical value in charting new directions for the design and operation of the executive process in the United States. Disillusionment with the effectiveness of ordinary hierarchical structures has been widespread in American politics in recent years. This dissatisfaction has been reflected in the efforts to allow clients to participate in the administration of poverty programs and to decentralize the structure of school systems and other community organizations.

In spite of these stirrings toward revisionism in organization theory, however, official reports and studies such as the Ash Council recommendations to President Nixon continue to propose reforms along traditionally hierarchical lines. If the Ash proposals for consolidating the activities of the seven major domestic departments into four super-departments were to be adopted, the amount of hierarchy in the national executive establishment would be enormously increased.

The conclusions of this study set our sights in quite a different direction than hierarchy. They demonstrate the feasibility of achieving cooperation among executive departments without necessarily resorting to hierarchical coordination. Where agencies can identify and develop complementary interests, they can be expected to cooperate without overhead direction and control.

Thus, this study of organizational exchange supports the belief that there is no iron law of hierarchy requiring organizational centralization in order to overcome the adverse effects of multiplying government programs and organizations in contemporary society. It is not altogether unrealistic to count on arrangements for mutual assistance in an environment that has often seemed characterized by a fiercely competitive struggle for survival. In this way, Professor Davis expands our intellectual horizons as we grope for ways and means of making executive organizations more humane and responsive in an increasingly bureaucratic world.

Francis E. Rourke

Preface

I owe special thanks to Francis E. Rourke of The John Hopkins University, not only for writing the foreword, but for his help and criticism in all phases of this study. Robert L. Peabody deserves similar thanks, as does William H. Oakland, who reviewed the text with an economist's careful eye. Mrs. Joy Pankoff cheerfully typed three drafts of the manuscript. The Woodrow Wilson Foundation of Princeton, New Jersey supported the work with a fellowship, for which I am grateful. Finally, I owe a major debt to the many bureaucrats in Washington who generously answered my questions, showed me their files, and continue to send me news of their agencies' activities.

1 Introduction

When on July 20, 1969, Astronaut Neil Armstrong so deliberately stepped from the Apollo 11 lunar module to make his "great leap for mankind," he simultaneously made a great leap for the National Aeronautics and Space Administration and, in turn, for the Department of State. In bringing the lunar program to this dramatic climax, NASA had not only benefited science but American foreign policy as well.

The process of foreign policy formulation extends far beyond the State Department—that branch of the bureaucracy formally charged with the responsibility—to include certain activities of NASA, the Labor Department, and the Treasury as well as many other departments and agencies. In the process of making American foreign policy, the State Department seeks to utilize the resources of other departments. It obtains these resources through a complex process of bureaucratic exchange. The objective of this book is to explore the extent to which microeconomic theories of exchange can be used to understand the process of foreign policy formulation by the federal bureaucracy.

The Analytical Context

Exchange theories have always formed an undercurrent of political analysis. Plato believed that the state owed its origin to needs of its citizens for exchange.[1] The Pythagoreans defined justice as strictly reciprocal exchange. Aristotle rejected the harsher aspects of this *lex talionis*; he would temper the strict reciprocity according to the position and motivation of the parties.[2] Aristotle held that the proper functioning of exchange relationships bound the state together. By their own services, men should repay the services of others. Thomas Hobbes held that by a contract among themselves, men could escape the State of Nature. Each man would obey the Sovereign; in return the Sovereign would confer the benefits of government. The social contracts of Locke, Hume, and Rousseau are similarly based on exchange principles.[3]

In the nineteenth century Georg Simmel applied theories of exchange to analyze social relationships: "All contacts among men rest on the schema of giving and returning the equivalence." He goes on to note that social agreements can be enforced just as economic agreements. Whereas the economic system depends on legal sanctions, society depends on social sanctions. Simmel uses the term "gratitude" to characterize the tie that binds one man to another in a social relationship.[4]

In 1958 George Homans again advanced exchange theory as a useful approach to the study of society in an article in *The American Journal of Sociology* where he writes "Social behavior is an exchange of goods, material goods but also non-material goods, such as the symbols of approval or prestige." The process is characterized by cost, rewards, and profits.[5]

In this article and in the expanded version which soon followed in book form, Homans depended heavily on a comparative study of two bureaus conducted in the late 1940s by Peter Blau.[6] In observing the bureaus (employment services of the state and federal governments) Blau noted that the behavior of the staff could best be explained in terms of exchange. Focusing his study on the individual case worker as the unit of analysis, Blau observed that the social structure of the offices was characterized by a complex network of exchange relationships. This was contrary to the neat hierarchical structure that supposedly governed the staff's behavior. Both the official doctrine of the employment services and traditional Weberian sociology decreed that the bureaus be structured hierarchically. Superiors were to give instructions to subordinates, who then implemented them. Ambiguities were to be referred back up the chain of command to insure conformity to official policies. Indeed one bureau had a rule forbidding case workers from obtaining advice from their peers.

The situation Blau actually observed in the two bureaus, however, was quite different from the hierarchical structure officially prescribed. Rather than occasionally seeking advice outside their chain of command, the caseworkers did so habitually—usually from their office mates. The official hierarchical model was thus a myth. Each bureau was structured into a series of advice-exchanging pairs. Blau observed that the behavior of the case workers followed certain principles of microeconomics. The willingness of an experienced case worker to give advice followed the law of diminishing marginal utility. Social norms of the staff established prices for the services rendered. The advice-exchanging pairs bargained in a fashion analogous to that of bilateral monopolies engaged in negotiations.

While in his early work Blau's economic orientation is implicit, he later becomes quite explicit in applying theories of exchange developed by microeconomists. Blau leans heavily on *Economic Analysis* by Kenneth Boulding for the theoretical structure for his analysis.[7] Boulding has himself explored the applications of economic principles to the social sciences. In *Conflict and Defense* he presents a series of hypothetical problems that can be analyzed in terms of the exchange process. He explains conflict resolution using concepts of bargaining space in the static situation and the Richardson model process in the dynamic one. He approaches the issue of the viability of a state (or other institution) in terms of a model of spatial competition originally derived from the theory of the competition of firms in the market place. In international relations Boulding moves beyond an abstract discussion to show the model's implications for the analysis of spheres of influence, buffer states, and colonial aggrandizement.[8]

In a 1969 article, Ralph M. Goldman presents what he calls an "exchange, or transactional," model of political integration and arms control.[9] Using microeconomic techniques Goldman analyzes historic cases of disarmament and projects his findings onto the present international system. He foresees a "Pattern T" leading to global arms control once the nations of the world realize that war is an inefficient mode of foreign policy production.

In his discussion of political integration Goldman notes the need of a common "currency," the political analogue to the money currency in the economic sphere. Talcott Parsons previously noted the same need and observed that "power" is the currency of the political process.[10] James Coleman has proposed reforms in legislatures in an attempt to transform power into a convertible currency. The unit of political money would be the vote. The legislator would "spend" his vote just as a consumer spends his dollars.[11]

Voting lends itself to economic and mathematical analysis. One of the more renowned pioneers in this field was Lewis Carroll who wrote several pamphlets analyzing the paradoxes of majority rule.[12] Carroll thus balanced the satirical critique of parliamentary personalities given in *Alice in Wonderland* with this mathematical critique of parliamentary procedures.

In *The Calculus of Consent* Buchanan and Tullock developed a field they chose to name the "economic theory of constitutions."[13] In their model the citizen is an economic man who rationally decides to participate in a collective action according to the cost-benefit ratio. Mancur Olson treats a more limited aspect of this problem in *The Logic of Collective Action*.[14] Looking at the problems of labor unions, Olson observes that as the size of the group increases the collective benefits each member receives becomes less dependent on his own contribution. Hence many withdraw their support. In order to maintain its base of support the group must turn to coercion or to providing non-collective benefits to entice the members to stay.

An Economic Theory of Democracy[15] is a third book to follow this approach, known in the field as welfare economics. The author, Anthony Downs, examines the behavior of political parties and those who vote for them. The rational voter, seeking to maximize his utility, votes for the party most likely to meet this goal. The party in turn, seeking to maximize the number of votes it receives, pursues a strategy of offering an attractive utility income to a majority of the electorate.

Downs takes some of the concepts of information cost, decision making, and uncertainty used in this book to analyze mass voting and applies them to bureaucratic behavior in his second book, *Inside Bureaucracy*.[16] The author assumes that all bureaucrats are rational utility maximizers. Yet utility is a complex set of goals including power, income, prestige, security, loyalty, pride in excellent work, and desire to serve the public interest. Downs believes that bureaucratic behavior is subject to a set of sixteen laws, such as the law of increasing conservatism, the law of hierarchy, the law of ever expanding control and the power shift law. Unfortunately, the author fails to follow economic theories as closely in this book as in the first one. Indeed the economic analysis has been reduced to the point where it is little more than occasional references to bargaining, rationality, and utility.

Gordon Tullock encounters the same problem when he shifts his attention from voting to bureaucratic behavior. In writing *The Politics of Bureaucracy* Tullock is little more successful than Downs in applying economic theories to bureaucracy.[17] He does not go much beyond a few analogies to monopsony, contracts, and cost accounting.

One economist who has been more successful, though less self-conscious, in applying economic theories to the bureaucratic process is Charles Lindblom. Writing in *The Intelligence of Democracy* Lindblom sets forth a theory of "decision-making through mutual adjustment."[18] The author observes that most decisions made in a bureaucracy are not really hierarchical but are actually made by the various actors adjusting their behavior to each other. Independent, partisan decision makers can be coordinated without a central coordinator. Sometimes this is done without the actors involved even responding to each other directly. More often it is done through a process of negotiation.

Lindblom's decision-making orientation is shared by the authors of a book examining the possibilities of an economic approach to decision making in underdeveloped nations. Ilchman and Uphoff cast themselves in the imaginary role of advisors to General Gowan of Nigeria.[19] They then proceed to offer the general advice on how to run his country, based on economic analysis of political problems. Ignoring the established meaning of the term, they call their approach political economy. Although marred by a dearth of actual, rather than hypothetical, examples, the book is a worthy attempt to apply economic theory to the total range of a nation's politics. The authors posit the polity to be composed of a series of sectors. The sectors are basically equivalent to interest groups: landlords, peasants, the military, the intellectuals, the church, etc. The government regime exchanges resources with the various sectors, sometimes giving and other times taking.

Levine and White have examined the exchange of resources among public health agencies. The agencies studied exchanged knowledge, funds, and services. The authors define exchange in terms of goal realization. Among other things this means that "the action may be unidirectional and yet involve exchange."[20]

To satisfy an apparently growing market for the application of economic theories to politics Curry and Wade have written a brief introductory textbook. It attempts to present the essential principles that might be most appropriate for political analysis. The authors twin goals of breadth and brevity are admirable, but the combination results in a superficial treatment of the field. The essentials are there but in a form so condensed that the novice cannot comprehend them. At the same time one familiar with the economic theories presented will find the book too elementary. The author's second venture is more satisfactory. Abandoning the pseudosimplification of the first, the second book presents and discusses at a more advanced level a series of seven microeconomic aspects of politics.[21]

A second stream of political analysis which, like the economic undercurrent, has recently emerged is the explanation of policy formulation in terms of bureaucratic actors. Paul Hammond, Morton Halperin, and Graham Allison have all viewed foreign policy from this approach.

In "Foreign Policy Making and Administrative Politics" Hammond asserts that the focus of policy making has shifted increasingly from the "public governmental sector" (Congress and the president) to the "privileged governmental sector" (the bureaucracy).[22] Thus to understand foreign policy formulation the political scientist must examine the bureaucratic process. This process is characterized by bargaining among the various bureaucratic actors in the policy arena.

Halperin has taken a complementary approach. He views bilateral international relations as the interaction of two bureaucracies.[23] Neither nation is a unitary actor. Nor is the bureaucracy of each unitary. Each bureaucracy is a composite of various departments, bureaus, and offices interacting with one another to produce a series of policies, known in the aggregate as the government's foreign policy. Any speech is a compromise. Any action is a compromise. The various bureaus seek conflicting goals. In their competition with each other agencies overstate their positions, ignore contradictory information, and even sabotage other agencies. Halperin opines that most messages sent to influence foreign bureaucracies have no effect whatsoever. The target bureau abroad is too inflexible to respond. Changes are more likely to come about because of internal shifts of power within the foreign bureaucracy.

Taking the 1962 Cuban missile crisis as a case study, Allison notes that most political analysts explain (and predict) the behavior of national governments in terms of rational, unitary policy formulation.[24] Like Hammond and Halperin, Allison believes the unitary model (which he designates Model I) to be inadequate. He presents two alternatives: II, an organizational process model, and III, a bureaucratic politics model. Model II views policy as the "outputs of large organizations functioning according to standard patterns of behavior." The actor is the department, bureau or office, which goes about producing its share of the total policy in an environment of parochialism and routine. Limited flexibility and incremental change characterize the organizational model. Model III views policy as the resultant of bargains struck among key personalities in the bureaucracy. The actor to be analyzed is a man holding a position of influence. The behavior of these men is a product both of their roles and of their personalities. The Secretary of State was Mr. State Department but he was also Dean Rusk. The Senior Senator from New York was the President's Chief Republican Critic but he was also Kenneth Keating. The outcome is a function of the positions occupied by the key actors and of their ability to build coalitions.

The third stream of analysis now emerging is a policy orientation. Like the previous two, economic and bureaucratic, this approach has attracted increasing attention in recent years. Theodore Lowi's 1964 book review in *World Politics* is frequently cited as the seminal article.[25] Here Lowi proposed to reverse the former priorities in policy analysis. The old order had decreed that policy content was the dependent variable; and process, the independent variable. Lowi proposed to consider the policy content as the independent variable. The particular structuring of policies varies among the assorted analysts. Lowi advanced a three part categorization to describe policy systems: distributive, regulatory and redistributive. Robert Salisbury added a fourth: self-regulative.[26] Lewis Froman has garnered five other abstract policy categories from the literature: (1) style-position, (2) symbolic-material, (3) strategic-structural, (4) areal-segmental, and (5) zero-sum—non-zero-sum.[27] While the different policy analysts all advance different sets of categories by which to describe the policy formulation process, all agree to reversing the priorities so that the content will be emphasized and the process deemphasized. In terms of the scope of the field to be analyzed the policy analysts take a middle ground between consideration of a general process and consideration of a specific case. Thus an orientation toward content leads to the study of a policy arena.

The Institutional Context

The analytical context points toward the study of a policy arena conceived in terms of bureaucratic units interacting according to economic principles. The policy is foreign policy—more specifically foreign policy with respect to labor, space, and finance. The units of analysis are the State Department, the Labor Department, the National Aeronautics and Space Administration and the Treasury—more specifically the international affairs branches of each of the three domestic departments and the State Department bureaus that interact with them.

The three sub-arenas of foreign policy—labor, space, and finance—represent three distinct types of politics. Labor displays a traditional interest group pattern. It is representative of other traditional political interaction matrices such as those of agriculture, business, and veterans affairs. Space, in contrast, displays a nontraditional, technical orientation. The NASA pattern offers a possible preview of a future style of technocratic politics. Finance presents a third and different pattern. To some extent it follows an interest group pattern like labor; to some extent it is technocratic like space. Yet to these it adds an element of its own. Finance, focusing as it does on vast sums of money, often transcends its own sub-arena to overwhelm the entire foreign policy process.

The linkage between the State Department and the three domestic departments is symmetrical. Each of the domestic departments has a bureau specializing in international affairs. This bureau in turn deals primarily with a bureau of the State Department which in a reciprocal fashion is established to form a contact point on that department's side. Labor's Bureau of International Labor Affairs handles contacts with the State Department via that department's Office of Labor Affairs. NASA's Office of International Affairs deals with State's Bureau of International Scientific and Technological Affairs. The Treasury's International Affairs branch deals with State's Bureau of Economic Affairs. The perfect symmetry is embellished in the actual day to day operations. The ILAB regional desk officers deal directly with the regional labor advisors in State's five geographic bureaus. NASA's International Office deals with State's U.N. Office on matters affecting the United Nations. NASA has also "spun off" some programs. The space agency developed communications satellites, but NASA shed the program once it became operational. The Comsat Corporation now has that responsibility. In the future NASA plans to shed additional programs now in the developmental stages. The State Department's tenuous absorption of the Agency for International Development and the U.S. Information Agency further elaborates the basic pattern. Although officially part of the State Department establishment, neither AID nor the USIA is fully integrated. With a few exceptions AID maintains a separate identity. Labor affairs is one of those exceptions. The same Labor Office serves both the parent department and its constituent agency. The USIA is even more distinct than AID. It maintains an entirely parallel structure.

The Labor Department is further linked to the State Department through the labor attaché program. The attachés are Foreign Service Officers attached to the embassies abroad as specialists in labor affairs. As FSOs these men are members of the Foreign Service. While the Foreign Service is officially the joint undertaking of the departments of State, Labor, and Commerce, in fact the State Department orientation predominates since the labor attachés make up only a tiny fraction of the total corps. Their selection, training, and promotion is a joint responsibility. The benefits of their services go to both departments. The State Department seeks the more general political and economic expertise. The Labor Department is more concerned with specific labor issues. The Treasury has representatives attached to sixteen embassies, but unlike the labor attachés, the Treasury representatives are not in the Foreign Service. The Treasury prefers that its men remain independent of the State Department.

Exchange

The foreign policy arena, insofar as it is exemplified by the behavior of the four departments under consideration, is organized on the basis of exchange. The essentials of a simple exchange process are at least two parties and at least two commodities for them to trade. The first bureau gives commodity x to the second. In return the second bureau gives commodity y to the first.[28] The ratio at which the two bureaus exchange commodities is the price.[29] Economists classify the economic actors which are parties to exchange into three categories: (1) original suppliers, (2) intermediaries, and (3) ultimate demanders.[30] Ultimate demanders are consumers—individual persons usually organized into family households. Original suppliers and intermediaries may be individual persons, but more typically in a complex economy they are firms. In the policy formulation process the three categories often merge. A bureau is simultaneously an original supplier, an intermediary, and an ultimate demander. Indeed this happens in the economic process as well. A farmer will grow corn, buy hogs to fatten them for resale, and buy food to feed his own family. In an analogous fashion a bureau will manufacture a certain commodity, transmit another commodity as an intermediary, and consume a third commodity.

Specialization is a prerequisite of exchange. Without specialization each economic actor would produce the same commodity, hence there would be no reason to exchange. But with specialization each produces a different commodity more efficiently because of economies of scale and greater skill. Then through exchange each can obtain the commodities of the other. The total economy has raised its productivity.[31] Within the foreign policy arena specialization has long been taken for granted. Each bureau produces its own commodities which it then exchanges with other bureaus for the commodities produced by those bureaus. Indeed this principle has found its way into law in the Foreign Assistance Act of 1961 which provides that the State Department obtain the services of the domestic departments in the areas of agriculture, education, labor, etc.[32]

These basic principles of exchange, however, are only the beginning of an analysis of the more complex forms in both economics and bureaucratic politics. More than two parties may be involved. In the early days of the American republic Yankee merchants grew rich on the infamous "triangular trade": New England rum to Africa for slaves, slaves to the West Indies for sugar, sugar to New England for rum. In a similar fashion the Labor Department supplies services to the State Department which in turn furnishes services to organized labor which completes the triangle by giving political support to the Labor Department.

A second complication arises from the .time span of the exchange. The simplest exchanges are consummated at once. Both parties give and receive at the same time. But in more complicated exchanges the reciprocity is less obvious. The exchange process is characterized by a flow of commodities rather than a *quid pro quo* barter. A large corporation views its exchanges as flows of commodities. General Motors cannot price an automobile on the costs of manufacturing that particular vehicle because it does not know its costs for the individual item. Instead it estimates a "mark up" based on the overall costs of production. GM does not know its financial situation until it calculates a quarterly balance sheet. Even this is based on the unending flows of commodities from its suppliers, dealers, etc.

In a like manner government bureaus view their exchanges with each other in terms of flows rather than *quid pro quo* trades. NASA performs certain services for the State Department and the State Department performs other services for NASA. But the commodities are not exchanged on a one to one basis. NASA may perform one big service while State performs a series of small ones in return. The State Department may give commodities to NASA one year to be reciprocated by NASA the next year. Since all the agencies are continually engaged in a multitude of exchanges at the same time, one commodity is seldom viewed as specific repayment of another. Rather the agencies are concerned with insuring that the total flow of commodities is satisfactory.

That the foreign policy formulation process is one of commodity flows testifies to its dynamic character. Yet much recent analysis of the field had stressed a deterministic approach. Chris Argyris asserts that the State Department is moribund because it is staffed by conservative, inhibited, and unimaginative men. The cautious diplomats produce a cautious agency.[33] John Harr paints a similar picture. The typical FSO is conservative, status-conscious and conformist; the corps reflects these traits.[34] Andrew Scott believes that the State Department suffers from the malaise of spirit in its ranks. Its old line officers have resisted the modernization of the department. It has neglected to develop the potential of contemporary political research.[35] The essence of the arguments of this sort is that the current situation in the foreign policy arena is the result of prior, and basically unalterable, factors. If a policy is a certain way, it is because the FSOs are the particular personalities that they are.

In contrast an economic approach views policies as equilibrium positions resulting from the dynamic interaction of the various agencies in the arena. American policy with respect to foreign astronauts is what it is because that is the present equilibrium position between the State Department, NASA, and other agencies acting in the arena. American policy on the balance of payments is the current equilibrium between State, the Treasury, etc. These policy positions are not preordained by the recruitment and socialization of personnel but by the pulling and hauling of agencies in the bureaucratic market place. Deterministic analysis cannot be entirely rejected; it has a useful function to serve. But the deterministic approaches too often result in a conclusion that provides little help in understanding a fluid situation. To say that the State Department is sluggish because its officers are conservative does little to explain how sluggish or how this will affect the formulation of a particular policy. This can be done better with an approach oriented toward the dynamics of the process.

Methodology

The purpose of this book is to examine the foreign policy formulation process in its typical form. Accordingly data was sought on the routine behavior of the bureaucracy. The facts are mundane. They represent the ordinary day to day interaction of the State Department with the domestic departments. They are not crises; they are seldom even newsworthy. Instead they are the plain grist of the foreign policy mill. This study does not attempt to judge whether the policy process follows a similar pattern in times of stress and crisis.

The international bureaus of the three domestic departments—Labor, NASA, and the Treasury—were selected for study, as mentioned before, because they represented three diverse political styles: interest group, technocratic, and financial. These three were among the seventeen bureaus previously studied in terms of their appropriations history.[36] All three had enjoyed rapid growth between 1957 and 1968. All three were small enough to be researchable.

The level chosen for investigation is best described as upper career.[37] This is just below the assistant secretary level. This level was selected in order to get at routine policy formulation. The officials interviewed were preponderantly career personnel. While many displayed a vivid awareness of partisan political considerations, none revealed a close affiliation with a political party. These men did not overtly owe their jobs to the party in power.

The data for the study came from interviews, direct observations, and documents. The total population interviewed numbered about thirty. In the three domestic departments this meant interviewing a major portion of the total personnel at the upper career level; in the State Department it meant covering a much smaller fraction. All interviews were face to face. The first set of questions focused on the respondent's own job, especially as it involved dealing with the counterpart department. The next were about other activities in his own or the other department. This was a check on the data from the other interviews. The final set of questions inquired specifically about relations with the counterpart bureau in terms of exchange. The officials were asked to comment on a list of twenty-three commodities. The officials questioned displayed courtesy, candor, and competence. They also displayed present-mindedness. They talked only of their current projects. When asked about events of one or two years previous they become vague, uncertain, and imprecise as to the temporal aspects. While they could recall a particular episode clearly, they would be unable to give its date accurately. Many spoke of events long past as if they had occurred recently.

At the beginning of an interview each respondent was promised that his identity would remain confidential for a five year period. Accordingly none are mentioned in the text by name, title, or distinctive characteristic in a way which would lead to their being coupled with information given in the interviews.

Initial contact with a bureau was made through a personal reference where possible. Otherwise the bureau's public information officer was approached. Once interviewing began respondents were asked to recommend other officials in their sub-arena. The interview process was itself an exchange. The officials gave information in return for a chance to present their side of the story. They also received deference from the interviewer. Blau notes that a subordinate gives deference when he has nothing else to give.[38] The respondents readily accepted the interviewer as an "insider" with whom they could share privileged information. This acceptance seemed to stem from two sources. First the interviewer displayed roughly the same professional, educational, and social characteristics as their colleagues. At the same time he was nonthreatening. He was young, academic, and transitory, hence no hazard to them.

Some of the data was obtained through direct observation. Erving Goffman has written that "the 'true' or 'real' attitudes, beliefs and emotions of the individual can be ascertained only indirectly . . ."[39] A few of the most revealing remarks were those overheard during telephone conservations that occasionally interrupted the questioning. Again being an "insider" helped. Subtle difference in presentation can only be appreciated by one familiar with the cultural milieu.

Documents formed the third source of data. Because of their comprehensiveness, congressional hearings are the greatest reservoir of information. Others are publication of the four departments. Still other information is from unpublished documents in the files of the bureaus studied. Finally, of course, some data was available in books, periodicals and newspapers.

A Preview

Commodities are the first building blocks in the exposition of an exchange analysis. While the commodities of economic intercourse are widely recognized, their bureaucratic counterparts are more obscure. Chapter 2 presents the bureaucratic commodities ordered in a continuum according to the degree to which they are transformed in the exchange process, beginning with those not changed and moving to those most changed. This is not an absolute categorization. To some extent it is an heuristic framework for presenting the commodities. But it does follow an underlying rationale which finds enhanced meaning in later discussions of bureaucratic production.

The next chapter considers one aspect of the commodities valuation: the utility function. This valuation is subjective. It is based on the utility of the commodity to the agency. The utility differs among the various agencies studied according to taste and quantity possessed. Unequal valuations by the actors leads to exchange. Indifference curve techniques used in analyzing utility have applications in the selection of foreign sites for meetings or facilities.

An agency specializes, as noted in Chapter 4, in order to gain the benefits of exchange. By specializing in the commodities that it can produce most efficiently and trading these with other agencies, it can maximize its resources. The form of this specialization can be determined by a number of factors: by other government agencies in Washington or overseas, by private institutions, by professional disciplines, by geography, by language, or by the level of production. The advantages of specialization, however, are mirrored by the disadvantages of segmentation. Each specialty isolates itself. The system becomes disjointed.

The fifth chapter examines the issue of jurisdiction. Each of the four departments studied has a bureaucratic territory of its own. The State Department has foreign affairs, the Labor Department has labor, NASA has space, and the Treasury has finance. The behavior of the departments with respect to this territory follows a pattern noted by economists in their studies of monopolies. The departments fight jurisdictional skirmishes along their borders and compete for dominion over newly opened territory.

Chapter 6 examines bargaining between the State Department and the domestic departments. This transpires in a number of different market places ranging from formal, highly structured, inter-agency committees to informal, transitory networks of contacts between officials operating within the same commodity set. Some agencies have developed bureaus specializing in the bargaining process. Others rely on each component to undertake its own negotiation. The bargaining strategies employed by the agencies fall into two sets: rules of consensus and rules of conflict. This dichotomy may be illuminated in terms of an Edgeworth Box. A bureau's choice of a consensus or a conflict strategy corresponds to its position on or off the Paretian optimum running from one corner of the box to the opposite one. A bureau will adjust its strategy according to whether its position is optimal or sub-optimal.

Production, the subject of the next chapter, is the process of increasing the value of a commodity. Bureaucratic production is grouped in categories compatible with those used in the exposition of commodities in chapter 2. Brokerage is productive because it puts the commodities where they are most demanded. In searching out bids and offers, then bringing them together, the broker moves commodities into the uses where they are most highly valued. The next two forms of production, assemblage and refining, are more akin to the popular notion of production. They are forms of bureaucratic manufacturing. Innovation, the fourth category of production, is productive because it creates new commodities where none existed before.

Chapter 8 deals with price. This ratio of exchange between the various commodities traded is much more elusive in the bureaucracy than in the economy. Occasionally it is explicit, particularly when money is one of the commodities being exchanged. But the overt exchange of funds is no guarantee that money is really the bureaucratic price. The terms of an exchange of funds may be more important than the amount. Price is determined by the market, which may be atomistic or monopolistic. The price system fulfills two functions: the first is to clear the market in the short run. The demand of bureaucratic commodities must be matched with the supply. The second is to allocate resources in the long run. This second function has led to the emergence of bureaucratic arbitrageurs and speculators.

The ninth chapter begins by examining the effect of agency attempts to allocate resources over time. This is a process of bureaucratic investment. Present consumption is foregone in order to increase future resources. Insurance may be contrasted with investment. The former seeks to maximize utility while the latter seeks to maximize wealth. The four departments studied seem more prone to insure than to invest.

The final chapter reappraises the problem which began this book: to what extent can microeconomic theories of exchange be used to understand the process of foreign policy formulation by the federal bureaucracy. As might be expected the verdict is favorable. Then, after suggesting some topics for further research, this chapter briefly considers the implications of exchange analysis for bureaucratic reform. To its own detriment the State Department has inappropriately clung to a hierarchical model. In its own reform proposals it has frequently advocated more rather than less hierarchy. The exchange model offers a better alternative both for the State Department and for American foreign policy in general.

Commodities

The commodities involved in bureaucratic exchange can range from the moon rocks brought back by Apollo 11 to new schemes of taxation invented by the Internal Revenue Service and from the weekly packet of newspaper clippings sent to the labor attachés to the negotiating position of the American delegation to an international conference. A commodity, as used here, is a generic term to describe anything that is exchanged. Economists often use "goods and services" as an alternative catchall phrase for commodities, but, as Kenneth Boulding points out, all goods are, in an ultimate sense, a bundle of services.[1]

The myriad commodities traded between bureaus may be arranged on a continuum according to the degree to which the commodities are transformed. This has been done in figure 2-1. The degree of transformation refers to the change in structure which the commodities undergo. It is analogous to the transformation of iron ore into steel or of steel into automobiles. The commodities fall roughly into four groups. First are those basic commodities not transformed but merely transmitted with little or no change in their form. Second are those commodities which are assembled. They undergo some transformation. They are sorted, combined, or rearranged. Third are those which are extensively transformed. The output is much different from the input. These are referred to as refined. Finally, those commodities most transformed—farthest to the right on the continuum—are described as invented. In this group the transformation has been so extensive that in final output bears little resemblance to the input.

Low Degree of Transformation	Group 1	Group 2	Group 3	Group 4	High Degree of Transformation
	Basic Commodities	Assembled Commodities	Refined Commodities	Invented Commodities	

Figure 2–1.

Group 1: Basic Commodities

The first group of basic commodities transmitted with little or no transformation includes such diversities as goods and services, raw information, personnel, funds, votes and vetoes, licenses and credentials, and guarantees of professional standards. The lunar samples represent an archetype of those commodities which are transmitted unchanged. NASA transferred seven to the USIA for one year—six for traveling exhibits abroad and one for the U.S. pavilion at Osaka's Expo 70. At the end of the year the seven samples remained unchanged. Other samples went to the White House thence President Nixon dispatched them as gifts to the chiefs of state of the 127 nations with which the United States has diplomatic relations.

Though less dramatic than the lunar samples, office space in the embassies is a commodity more frequently traded between the State Department and the other agencies represented abroad. The State Department provides administrative support for these agencies in the field. At each foreign capital the embassy administrative officer and the ranking officer of the agency negotiate an annual agreement on exactly how many square feet, desks, automobiles, etc., that agency will be entitled to. At the same time in Washington, a State Department administrator negotiates a general agreement with the agency's Washington headquarters on the terms of support world wide. In this sense then the State Department is like a chain of Hilton Hotels offering, for a price, to provide rooms and services to other governmental agencies.

The most popular of those services is transmitting messages.[2] The State Department operates an extensive courier system carrying the diplomatic pouches between the embassies and Washington. For more rapid communication the embassies are connected to Washington by a radio network capable of transmitting encoded messages. The agencies constantly use the State Department communication channels. A Foreign Service courier "pouches" manuscripts on space biomedicine between NASA and the Soviet space agency. Routine reports of the Treasury representatives arrive via the pouch. More urgent ones are cabled. The disadvantage with the cables is that they are not private. Foggy Bottom must approve the outgoing cables and reads the incoming ones before passing them on to the addressees. To maintain privacy the agencies can write directly to their representative in the field, thereby shortcircuiting the State Department.

Occasionally the domestic agencies need extensive amounts of space abroad. The Labor Department holds regional labor attaché conferences every three to five years. It needs hotel rooms, auditoriums, conference rooms, etc. The host embassy arranges for the Labor Department to rent the space in excess of what it can supply. Of the three agencies, NASA has the greatest demand for real estate. It needs sites for tracking and communication, for landing rights in airports to support missions, for recovery areas, and for the use of various rocket ranges. Since, as in the case of hotel rooms, the embassy does not have those commodities, its first task is to acquire them so they can be transmitted to the domestic agency. The requirements for NASA sites are so complex that the embassy does not handle the negotiations alone but works in conjunction with NASA personnel familiar with the technical requirements.

Technical publications are a frequently exchanged commodity. The Labor Department's Bureau of Labor Statistics publishes a series of monographs on labor law and practice abroad covering over forty countries ranging from Iceland to Panama and from Afghanistan to Japan. It also publishes a monthly report entitled *Labor Developments Abroad* and a magazine, *International Labor*. The Treasury publishes a semi-annual report of the foreign credits by the U.S. government. The Bureau of Customs offers publications to guide the importer or exporter. NASA publishes scores of technical reports and manuals of interest to other agencies and foreign governments.

Government manuals are only one form in which information is exchanged. From the outside a publication is an object—so many hundred pages with a brown cover—which some other agency or foreign government wants. From the inside it is a highly refined product of a team of experts. This is one sort of information. Another is the information gathered overseas and funneled into parent agencies at Washington as the raw material from which they produce manuals, reports, statistics, etc. This type of raw information is introduced here in Group 1 because it is transmitted basically unchanged. Labor attachés devote much of their time to gathering the raw data on wages, unemployment, and productivity which they send via State Department channels to the Bureau of Labor Statistics where the data is eventually transformed into statistics on the labor situation in those countries. Similarly, the sixteen Treasury representatives and the Foreign Service economic officers transmit raw data on finance to the Treasury for analysis. Such numbers, before they become statistics, are the clearest examples of raw information. The group includes verbal information as well. Facts are a commodity. The State Department's life blood is news. For the more dramatic news, the State Department's reporting network runs a poor second to the newspapers. The Associated Press, United Press International, and Reuters report major events many hours before the embassies are able to. But the wire services ignore the less dramatic news. The embassies devote much time toward the patient and systematic gathering of facts wanted by the various government agencies in Washington. A labor attaché sends the names of new officers in a Latin American trade union. A Treasury representative reports on a revised banking law in Germany. A science attaché in Japan notes a new advance in electronics. These individual bits of news are forwarded to Washington for analysis by the agency concerned. While there is no clear boundary between raw information and information in more refined form, the different stages of information are different commodities for purposes of exchange.

Airline highjackings are a spectacular example of personnel as a commodity. In September 1970 the Palestinian guerrilla organization, Al Fatah, exchanged passengers for prisoners held in British, German, and Swiss jails. Less spectacular personnel exchanges occur between the State Department and the three domestic agencies. In 1961 the State Department began assigning four or five Foreign Service Officers (FSOs) to the International Affairs Office of NASA. In 1966

NASA made the exchange reciprocal by assigning one of its employees to the State Department's Science Bureau.[3] The program terminated in 1970. The exchange was based on the concept of cross-training. The personnel exchanged were fully integrated into the work of their host agency. One official who participated in the program described the benefits in a series of pairs. He learned the business of his host agency and he also got an overview of his own agency which he did not have before. He learned the importance of NASA's program to foreign relations and the importance of foreign relations to NASA. He learned the need for interagency coordination and the techniques for achieving it. His host agency benefited during his tour from the expertise he brought with him. His parent agency benefited during the tour from having its own man in the other agency and after the tour from the new skills he brought back.

The Treasury's program with the State Department has been more limited. For a time the State Department assigned FSOs to be assistants to the Assistant Secretary of the Treasury for International Affairs. The program was not reciprocal. The Treasury did not have enough people to spare for assignment to Foggy Bottom. Indeed the Treasury persuaded several of the FSOs sent over to them to stay permanently. Treasury officials were not enthusiastic about the program. They considered it a device for training FSOs with few benefits for their department.

The Labor Department has the most complex set of personnel exchanges with the State Department. These range from borrowing an FSO for a few months to the life-long commitment of a labor attaché. Like the other government agencies, the Labor Department borrows FSOs for assignment in regular department jobs. These FSOs are usually labor attachés serving their Washington assignment. A typical assignment would be in the International Labor Affairs Bureau (ILAB) as a desk officer specializing in a geographic area. The ILAB has five of these area specialists in its Office of Country Programs. Each covers labor developments in his geographic area, dealing with other offices of the ILAB, other Labor Department bureaus, and the labor advisors and desk officers at the State Department.

The labor attaché program is the biggest and most important Labor-State exchange. Approximately sixty attachés and assistant attachés are assigned to the embassies. In those countries where no attaché is assigned a labor reporting officer covers labor developments. Labor is a recognized career specialty within the Foreign Service. An FSO choosing to specialize in it is thus entering into a long term interdepartment exchange program. The labor attaché remains in the Foreign Service; he does not transfer to the Labor Department. Yet because so much of his job, while administered by the State Department, is done on behalf of the Labor Department he is often under the effective control of the Labor Department.

In contrast to the lifetime exchange commitment of the labor attaché, agencies may exchange personnel for as short a time as a few hours. Embassies are eager to arrange for NASA scientists to speak to foreign audiences. An astronaut makes the most glamorous speaker, but, as one USIA administrator stated, "Any NASA official who has played a key role in the space effort is useful to us abroad." Short term personnel are the chief commodity in organizing delegations to international meetings. A financial conference requires Treasury personnel. A labor meeting requires Labor Department personnel and trade economists, and a conference on space requires NASA scientists.

Personnel as a commodity has two sides: people and positions. A major portion of the effort of interdepartmental coordination revolves around matching the people to the positions. The number of people tends to lag behind the number of slots, so most of the bargaining goes on over the issue of the slots. The people already in the program may serve as a floor limiting a reduction in the number of positions. A reduction which exceeds the normal attrition rates means that positions must be found for the excess personnel. The difficulties in bringing new personnel into a program seldom acts as a ceiling on expansion of the number of positions. Positions, not being flesh and blood with all the attendant problems, tend to be an easier commodity to trade than the actual men and women who fill these positions.

President Nixon's personnel cutback is being severely felt by the labor attaché program. This policy, code-named "Operation Reduction," was actually begun in the last year of the Johnson administration. Within the Foreign Service the onus of Operation Reduction has fallen on the Foreign Service Reserve Officers (FSRs). Since many of the labor attachés are FSRs the labor program has borne the brunt of the cutback. Whereas ten years ago the ILAB foresaw an overall expansion of the program limited only by the number of qualified personnel who could be trained, today it is losing established labor attaché posts.[4]

A number of those questioned about personnel exchanges stated that the personnel involved were second rate. No agency would send its best men. Those sent tended to be mediocre men who would not be missed by the parent agency. This observation meshes with the finding of John Ensor Harr that the "best" FSOs avoid specialization. The ambitious young FSO learns early that the political career path leads to an ambassadorship and so he strives to stay in the main stream.[5] Specialization in finance, science, and especially labor, is the kiss of death. Even economics, which is the chief alternative to the political route, is distinctly in second place. On the other hand, this characterization of exchanged personnel as mediocre was not expressed by all, nor did it seem necessarily to fit. The alleged ineptitude of the personnel exchanged may well have been caused by their inexperience, the very factor which the program was designed to overcome. In any case, the personnel exchange programs are on the decline. All three agencies have terminated any active program of direct personnel exchange with the State Department. The labor attaché program of indirect exchange is under attack by Operation Reduction.

Personnel exchanged between agencies are paid according to arrangements determined at the time the exchange was negotiated. In some cases they are paid directly by their host agency. AID is particularly devoted to this procedure of direct hire. The employee is given a leave of absence by his parent agency and hired by AID under the same sort of contract he would have if he were recruited from outside the government. In other cases the employee continues to be paid by his parent agency which is reimbursed by his host agency. NASA-State Department exchanges are on this basis. The parent agency continues to pay an official even though he may have worked at the other agency for several years. Technical experts assigned from the Labor Department to AID were paid in this way when they come under the DOLITAC program. DOLITAC is the acronyn for the Department of Labor International Technical Assistance Corps. It consists of twenty to thirty experts on labor permanently assigned to it. These are experienced men and women recruited from the Labor Department or from the trade union movement who intend to pursue a career abroad. The program includes a DOLITAC Reserve to provide experts for a single tour abroad. These DOLITACers work for AID but continue to be paid by the Labor Department. AID reimburses the Labor Department for their salary and expenses. Arrangements for labor attachés differ. Since the labor attachés are officers in the Foreign Service they are never really exchanged in terms of personnel arrangements. The State Department pays their salaries just as it does for all the other specialists in the Foreign Service.[6]

Funds for salary reimbursements and for other projects are one of the major commodities exchanged between agencies. In recent years the ILAB has been getting the majority of its funding through intragovernmental transfers. In fiscal year 1965 these funds jumped from the $300 thousand level to the $2-½ million level, an eight-fold increase. Intragovernmental funds now account for two-thirds of the ILAB's annual budget. The fiscal year 1970 budget agreement between the Labor Department and AID alone provided for the transfer of $1-¼ million.[7] None of the other three agencies derive nearly as high a level of support from intragovernmental transfers.

Money as a commodity exchanged between agencies is not confined to U.S. dollars. Many of the funds are foreign currencies. Since the mid-1960s the counterpart funds generated abroad by the sale of American agricultural products under provisions of Public Law 480 have been one of the bureaucratic commodities most actively traded. The federal departments carry on a lively commerce among themselves in Indian rupees, Polish zlotys, and Tunisian dinars.

NASA has taken a more direct course to get foreign money. It has solicited funds to support its space program from Canada, Japan, and European countries. Beginning in the fall of 1969 NASA Director Thomas O. Paine visited these countries to seek contributions.[8] This NASA initiative enjoyed the support of President Nixon and Congress. They liked the idea of foreign countries contributing to a program they viewed as international in its benefits. Since these countries are profiting from space technology it seemed appropriate that they should help pay for it with their marks, francs, and yen.

The next set of five commodities leads a double life. On one side, the five are a highly amorphous set of controls over the flow of other commodities which defy classification. On the other, they are the institutionalized forms of these controls so simplified and standardized that they are routinely exchanged without being transformed. For this reason they are introduced here. These institutionalized controls over the flow of other commodities are the votes and vetoes, licenses and credentials, and guarantees of professional standards which make up so much of the bureaucratic currency.

A number of interagency committees vote in a formal fashion. They meet, discuss their agenda, and vote on the issues they are to decide. The Board of the Foreign Service and its subsidiary boards are the best example.[9] The Foreign Service Board was reorganized and renamed by the Foreign Service Act of 1946 to provide interdepartmental control of the newly revamped interdepartmental Foreign Service. As the domestic agencies are fond of saying, "it is the Foreign Service *of the United States*, not of the State Department." The Agriculture and Commerce Departments were represented because their foreign representatives were being merged into the Foreign Service. In an attempt to enhance their position vis-à-vis the State Department these two domestic departments managed to gain an additional seat on the board for the Labor Department. Members of the board are at the assistant secretary level. Operating under the board and arousing much more day-to-day interest are the promotion boards. The Labor Department is represented on any board considering promotions for FSOs in the labor specialty. The ILAB takes great care in naming the Labor Department's representatives to the promotion boards. It seeks a board member skilled in committee negotiations who will be able to help labor attachés up the career ladder. The board member must boost the labor specialists but at the same time he must not appear to be purely a special pleader.

From time to time the Foreign Service Board establishes ad hoc groups. In 1970 Deputy Under Secretary of State William Macomber headed a self-evaluation by the State Department.[10] He organized thirteen task forces to evaluate different facets of foreign policy execution. The Labor Department appointed representatives to five of these task forces concerned with career assignments, training, recruitment, promotion, and the role of the diplomatic mission.

The National Advisory Council on International Monetary and Financial Policies is another example of an interdepartmental committee with formal voting. The members of the National Advisory Council are the Secretaries of the Treasury, State, and Commerce, the Chairman of the Board of Governors of the Federal Reserve System, and the President of the Export-Import Bank. Alternates are drawn from the assistant secretaries in these agencies.[11] The National Advisory Council never convenes at the secretarial level and seldom convenes at the assistant-secretarial level. Face to face meetings are held weekly at the "staff level." Each of the member agencies sends a representative. The international banking institutions send representatives when one of their transactions is being discussed. Area specialists from the Treasury and the State Department attend meetings when loans affecting their areas are on the agenda. The purpose of these meetings is to coordinate the international monetary policies of the different departments through a process of mutual adjustment. The NAC approves or disapproves transactions of the international banking institutions such as the Inter-American Development Bank and the Asian Development Bank. In the case of the World Bank and the International Monetary Fund (IMF), the NAC advises the Secretary of the Treasury on the position he should take. The duties of the NAC require frequent votes. On routine transactions the votes are cast by the staff level representative either at one of the regular meetings or by telephone for issues that come up between meetings. The NAC operates under less formal rules of procedure than the Foreign Service boards. In part this is because their jurisdiction is less. The assistant secretaries who sit on the Board of the Foreign Service want firm decisions regarding FSO promotions from the subordinate promotion boards. They do not want a personnel decision "bucked up" to them. Consequently decisions are worked out within each promotion board and each board member's vote is more definitive. In contrast, the assistant secretaries who sit on the NAC do not necessarily want firm decisions in controversial monetary policies. The staff level meetings of the NAC are to deal only with routine decisions; more sensitive issues such as the 1971 devaluation are to be decided at a higher level. Thus in the NAC a vote is a less definitive commodity. Being less definitive, it is harder to exchange.

A veto is a special sort of vote. It is a vote which must be obtained before an act can take place. Bureaucratic politics is full of such votes. All the approvals, concurrences and endorsements which a proposal must surmount are potential vetoes. Vetoes are a form of serial voting. An issue must get a *yes* vote from one after another agencies rather than all the agencies voting at once according to some less than unanimity rule. The NAC again serves as an example. Internally the NAC operates on a majority vote procedure (though often stressing consensus). But the issues which it is deciding are whether or not to veto the transactions of the international banking institutions. In the case of U.S. banks such as the Inter-American Bank and the Asian Bank, the NAC decision is complete. In the case of the World Bank and the IMF, their decision is in the form of a recommendation to the Secretary of the Treasury of what his action should be. The NAC frequently enters into an exchange of vetoes over time. From time to time the NAC wishes to veto a certain loan but finds it difficult to veto that specific loan because things have gone too far to stop. The NAC will refrain from vetoing that particular transaction but will threaten to veto any similar loans which that bank might propose. The NAC will set forth policy guidelines for future transactions.

Refusing to vote can equal a polite veto when that vote is necessary. In international banking arrangements with weighted voting the U.S. vote is often necessary for approval. The Inter-American Bank's Fund for Special Operations functions this way. Rather than veto a transaction outright, the United States may simply refuse to vote at all until suitable revisions are made.

The informal clearance of labor attaché assignments by the AFL-CIO national headquarters amounts to a veto. Particularly in the early days of the program, but even now, approval of the headquarters on 16th Street is necessary for incoming labor attachés and for shifts at key labor posts. The link between 16th Street and the State Department was until recently George P. Delaney, a staunch trade unionist who held the double job of Special Assistant to the Secretary of State and Director of the AID Office of Labor Affairs.[12] Delaney cleared the personnel assignments with the AFL-CIO, although, in the words of one labor attaché interviewed, "I don't think you would find any record."

Licenses and credentials are a second pair of commodities based on control over the flow of other commodities. License is the right to operate in the jurisdictional territory of another agency. Radio broadcast licenses are of this type. Within the United States the Federal Communications Commission has jurisdiction over those bands of the electromagnetic spectrum suitable for communications. A station wishing to broadcast applies to the FCC for a portion of the spectrum. In 1966 ESRO, the European Space Research Organization, applied to the FCC for permission to build a space tracking and communications station in Fairbanks, Alaska. ESRO wanted to track its satellites launched into polar orbit. It had asked NASA to track for them but NASA was only willing to do so on an "as available" basis. Since ESRO needed more dependability than this, it applied and received a license to build its own station.

International arrangements to allot the electromagnetic spectrum are vastly more complicated. Radio waves do not recognize national boundaries. In certain frequencies even a weak station can be heard around the world. International agreements have limited the frequencies which each government can license. In effect, the countries have collectively licensed each other. International conferences meet regularly to readjust this worldwide division of the radio spectrum. By the early 1960s scientists realized that the demands of space communications could not wait for the next regular conference so they arranged to call the 1963 Extraordinary Administrative Radio Conference in Geneva. The Americans, the Russians, and the Europeans all had different amounts and ranges that they wanted to use. Finally the EARC compromised. It reserved a two thousand kilocycle band for space use.[13]

Just as the FCC has jurisdiction over the radio spectrum, so do government agencies have jurisdictions of their own. The State Department has jurisdiction in foreign affairs; the Treasury, in finance; the Labor Department, in labor affairs; and NASA, in space. And just as the FCC licenses broadcasters, so government agencies license other agencies to operate within their jurisdictional territories. These licenses become commodities to be bargained and exchanged for other commodities. For example the Treasury wanted to send an assistant secretary abroad to negotiate with foreign governments regarding the management of U.S. dollar reserves which they held. The form in which these governments held dollar reserves could be manipulated to improve the U.S. balance of payments position. But since such a mission involved basic issues of foreign affairs the Treasury could not undertake it without the State Department's permission. The Treasury needed a license from the State Department to engage in diplomacy. In a similar case the Treasury wanted to send a representative to Europe to negotiate a military offset agreement. To do so it needed a license from the State Department.

In many ways credentials are the reciprocal of a license. Credentials are a legitimation by one agency of an activity of another. For a labor attaché to gain access to the labor movement of his host country he needs to have credentials from American labor. The foreign trade unionists must not think of him as a diplomat but as one sympatico with labor. Striped pants are bad and a cloth cap is good. To get this labor image the FSO gets credentials from the Labor Department and from the AFL-CIO. In the early post-war era many of the labor attachés were recruited from the trade union movement. These labor attachés had earned their own legitimacy by coming up through the ranks. But now the typical labor attaché is a young FSO who chooses a labor specialty. He has more need for the credentials. The Labor Department confers its legitimacy in two ways. First, it puts the novice labor attaché through a ten month training period. He becomes thoroughly familiar with the department and with the trade union movement. Secondly, the department continues to support him the rest of his career as a labor attaché. In its program of "backstopping," the department keeps the labor attaché informed, answers his requests, etc., to the point where he is more a functionary of the Labor Department than of the State Department. The AFL-CIO similarly legitimizes the labor attaché in two ways. First, the new labor attaché is invited to 16th Street for meetings with the national officers and staff. The smart labor attaché gets an autographed photograph of this comraderie for his future office. He also spends a two week internship in the field with a member union. Secondly, the AFL-CIO also "backstops" the labor attaché throughout his career.

Credentials are not always an easy commodity in which to deal. European finance ministry officials are reluctant to negotiate with State Department economists. They prefer talking to Treasury "bankers" who are more trustworthy in the serious matter of money. The FSO economist will always be tainted as a diplomat no matter how respectable his credentials in finance.

The last of the five commodities which are institutionalizations of control over the flow of other commodities is a guarantee of professional standards. It is the same guarantee which the legal profession gives to the public by maintaining high standards for admission to the bar or the state medical board gives by examining and licensing physicians. When a layman goes to a professional the system guarantees him minimum qualifications. This guarantee of professional competence is part of the service provided. The Treasury is quite aware of the importance of professional standards and of their own high reputation. Just as physicians decline to criticize their fellow practitioners, so the Treasury declines to give public judgments on other treasuries' actions. When the International

Affairs branch receives letters inquiring about the possibility of a currency's devaluation it answers with this standard reply:

It is not the policy of the U.S. Government to comment on the status of foreign currencies. One can readily understand that no government would wish to have any other government expressing judgments to private businessmen regarding the status of its currency and the likelihood of an exchange adjustment.[14]

Many interviewees from the Treasury mentioned that foreign bank and finance ministry officials respected their competence and preferred dealing with them to dealing with State Department economists. One cited an instance where the State Department itself chose to act through the Treasury representative in preference to its own man. Washington ordered the Treasury representative to prepare the country economic report rather than the Foreign Service economist on duty in the same embassy. In general, however, all the economists enjoy high esteem for their competence by their colleagues. Treasury officials respect the abilities of State Department economists and vice versa Mutual respect, however, is not the same as trust. Each department tends to be skeptical of the motives of the other. Neither department holds the other in awe. The State Department economists do not revere the Treasury as the source of financial wisdom as the Treasury claims outsiders are wont to do.

The undercurrent of subdued rivalry between economists in State and the Treasury did not repeat itself in the relationship between scientists in State and NASA. For one thing there are many fewer points of contact. State and Treasury economists encounter each other dozens of times a day. The State Department has so few scientists and NASA has so much less international business that a handful of men can handle all the routine liaison. A second reason for less rivalry is the nature of the two disciplines. In economics "facts" are subject to varying interpretations according to whose purposes are to be served. Astrophysics is more clear-cut. The various scientists usually agree on an answer. A third reason is that the State-NASA liaison does not really turn on scientific issues whereas the State-Treasury relation always turns on economic ones. State sees its role as supporting the NASA mission and exploiting its successes. It is inconceivable that the State Department could never enter into the issue of the basic scientific merits. But in economic questions the State Department is vitally concerned. State sees the Treasury as an instrument of U.S. foreign policy as much as it sees its role as supporting the Treasury mission. It is no wonder that the economists from the two departments often clash despite their professional brotherhood. The importance of a guarantee of professional standards as a commodity is weakened because in the past NASA has deemphasized its scientific side for its management side. This deemphasis of science has meant a deemphasis of professional standards. With the exception of manned missions where safety was involved, NASA has deliberately under-engineered its projects. The emphasis has been on speed of delivery. NASA has preferred to launch an unperfected system, nurse it along and learn by its mistakes, than to wait until all the potential defects are worked out. Indeed, the inquiries conducted after the fatal Apollo 1 fire and the Apollo 13 abort accused NASA of being nearly as careless with its manned missions.[15] Except for manned missions where lives are being risked, this NASA policy may be most rational. In the context of the space race with the U.S.S.R. and in view of the still fairly high success rate, under-engineering is probably the most efficient way to operate. In any case NASA has not been as concerned with the question of professional standards as the Treasury.

Neither the labor attaché nor the Labor Department official can offer much in the way of a guarantee of professional standards. Neither has access to a body of esoteric knowledge as does the Treasury economist or the NASA astrophysicist. Neither can manipulate reality through the application of his expertise. The Treasury economist can send the price of gold up or down and the NASA astrophysicist can send a rocket to the moon. The labor specialist cannot approach such deeds. Lacking a body of esoteric knowledge, the FSO or the Labor Department official seeks to substitute experience. The labor specialist values his years of adventures in union affairs the way the economist and the scientist value their own organized bodies of knowledge. Unfortunately for the labor specialist, he is not able to command the respect for his experience that the economist and the scientist have for their more organized disciplines.

As a supplementary commodity the FSO and the Labor Department official offer another type of guarantee of professional standards. This is their good character. The modern FSO makes a point of maintaining his professional integrity. He repudiates Sir Henry Wotton's quip that "an ambassador is an honest man who is sent to lie abroad for the good of his country."[16] Today's diplomat never lies, although he reserves the right to say that he does not know. Integrity is a service which the FSO offers when he enters negotiations.

For the Labor Department official the equivalent is devotion to the labor movement. Working class origin, blue collar employment and long-standing union membership evince this character. The ideal would be a man born into a poor family of coal miners who organized a local union and only entered government service after being blacklisted. That sort of character would be a five carat diamond in bureaucratic exchange.

The new FSO entering the labor field without a labor background needs to acquire this guarantee of professional standards in order to be an effective labor attaché in his future assignments. Fortunately, the Labor Department and the AFL-CIO have maintained a high standard in the selection. Prospective labor attachés are screened by both the Labor Department and the AFL-CIO for proper attitude and character. Their veto right helps assure that the labor attaché corps will be kept pure of "company men."

Group 2: Assembled Commodities

Moving to the right on the continuum, the second major group of commodities are those designated as assembled. The first group consisted of basic commodities, whether tangible or intangible, whose form remained unaltered in the exchange process. A moon rock remained a moon rock, and a vote remained a vote, even after being traded. This second group consists of commodities in an early stage of transformation. The component units remain the same but they are assembled into a different form as they flow through the various agencies. The term "assembled" is used in a generic sense. The commodities may actually be disassembled, sorted, combined or rearranged in the process.

Implicit in this continuum is a theory of bureaucratic manufacturing. In the first group the commodities remained unchanged by the exchange process, but in the second group the commodities undergo a transformation, however slight. In the first group the productivity of the agency consisted of distribution only, but in the second group the agencies manufacture a new commodity, at least insofar as assembly transforms the original input. Productivity, for commodities in the second group, consists of distribution plus elementary manufacturing.

The best example of an assembled commodity is the labor packet prepared by the ILAB for distribution to the labor attachés in the field. Physically, the labor packet is a manila envelope containing newspaper clippings, press releases, and ILAB handouts. A lightweight packet goes out weekly by air. A heavier one goes out biweekly by sea. The ILAB assembles the materials from fifty-five different publications ranging from the house organs of the trade unions to *U.S. News and World Report* and *Business Week* on the management side. News from the Labor Department and other government departments is included. As a commodity the packet represents the lowest level of bureaucratic manufacturing. The news clippings and handouts (which are themselves Group 1 commodities) are assembled into a new commodity: the labor packet.

Another exchange of an assembled commodity is the data which the State Department forwards to the Labor Department from the labor attachés reports. The labor attachés routinely send reports on local labor conditions to the State Department. At the State Department the labor advisor for the geographic bureau reads the cables and sorts out various items for further distribution both within and without the State Department. This sorting process produces a new commodity different from the input he started with.

This pattern of information assembly is repeated many times in other agencies. On what one respondent referred to as "the data front," information is collected and assembled by the Treasury, then sent to the Department of Commerce for analysis. Other information is collected and assembled by Commerce for the further use of the Treasury. NASA has a European representative stationed in Paris whose job is to collect and assemble technical information on space for transmission to headquarters. In other countries the technical intelligence is assembled by the embassies.

Oftentimes the domestic agencies do not realize beforehand what information will be valuable to them and have no system of gathering it. In these cases information assembly consists of recognizing a useful bit of information and plucking it out of the mass of irrelevant information. Labor attachés are always on the outlook for these scraps of information which will prove valuable to the

Labor Department or to some other domestic agency. For example, European trade unions are far ahead of their American counterparts in training youth. Apprenticeship programs began there long before they began in the United States. Today labor attachés can see first hand European successes which might be applied at home. Compared to the Treasury representative or the science attaché, the labor attaché faces a more difficult time in bringing a labor program back home. It is easier to transmit information on technical matters like finance or space than on social matters. Because social conditions differ, it is hard to introduce programs from abroad.

Visits by foreigners and trips by Americans abroad are assembled commodities. They are assembled in terms of consisting of air transportation plus a site to visit, plus a guide, plus hotel accommodations, plus entertainment, etc. The trip package is assembled from commodities of the Group 1 type. The visit most popular with foreigners is one to a NASA site. Cape Kennedy ranks first; the Houston Manned Flight Center is second. NASA handles many visitors at Goddard Space Flight Center because it is close to Washington. While presidents and premiers receive the publicity, science ministers are the more common visitors. They can better justify a visit than the run of the mill VIPs clamoring to go to Kennedy or Houston. Occasionally NASA arranges a group visit. It flew the United Nations Committee on the Peaceful Uses of Outer Space to Houston for a briefing on earth resources survey satellites after President Nixon proposed an ERS program in a speech to the General Assembly in the fall of 1969.[17] NASA, in conjunction with USIA, will arrange a complete American tour for a foreign correspondent specializing in science.

The Labor Department assembles visits for foreign labor leaders. The ILAB hosts between four and five hundred annually. In past years the number has run as high as eight hundred. Two-thirds come under AID sponsorship. The majority of these are trade unionists. One-third come under the auspices of State's Educational and Cultural Affairs Bureau. These are mostly high ranking government and union officials. The ILAB's Division of Trade Union Exchange Programs which administers the visits is closely associated with the AFL-CIO. Sixteenth Street was instrumental in establishing and staffing it.

After being invited by the labor attaché, the typical foreign visitor flies to Washington for briefings by the State Department and the Labor Department. After a few days he goes to St. John's College in Annapolis for the program of the labor workshop. The workshop presents him a certificate of attendance. For many a visitor, this certification is the only "diploma" he possesses. Once home he will display it proudly. From Annapolis the visitor goes to two or three cities to meet with trade union officials and observe local union activities. After a few days to rest and sightsee, the foreign labor leader is debriefed in Washington and flown home, hopefully with a more favorable impression of American democracy.

Trips by Americans abroad are commodities reciprocal to visits by foreigners.

As with visits, a trip consists of assembling the component Group 1 commodities of transportation plus site, plus guides, etc. Because it is the agency on the ground with the embassies, the State Department can offer this commodity just as in the previous example the Labor Department could offer a labor oriented visit domestically.

An astronaut tour is the most glamorous trip the State Department assembles. The Office of Protocol has the chief responsibility. In Washington the State Department brings together the support team including personnel from NASA and USIA, determines the funding, selects the itinerary, and obtains a Special Air Mission aircraft from the Air Force.[18] Meanwhile the embassies along the route arrange the local schedule, protocol, publicity, and support. With each stop limited to one day the timing must be exact. The astronauts literally swoop down, call on the chief of state to present him with some moon dust, motorcade through town, lay a wreath at the statue of a national hero, field questions at a televised press conference, and then fly away to their next stop. Assembling an astronaut tour is a demanding job.

The State Department arranges for scientific trips. It laid the groundwork for the NASA expedition to Mexico to view the 1970 solar eclipse. It arranges trips abroad for high ranking officials from NASA or any other government agency. Actually such travel-agency services do not occupy much of the State Department's efforts. Most agencies with frequent business abroad are quite able to maintain their own contacts and assemble their own trips. They generally prefer to, so as not to complicate their plans by dealing through the State Department. They tend to call upon the State Department and the embassies only in nonroutine cases when special problems arise.

A delegation to an international meeting is an assembled commodity. It is a version of an interdepartmental committee. The State Department "manufactures" a delegation by putting together personnel from the various agencies interested in the meeting. As the agency having jurisdiction in foreign affairs, the State Department has maintained an exclusive right to assemble delegations. An agency cannot send its own delegate who is not accredited by Foggy Bottom. On the other hand, the State Department's freedom in assembling delegations is sharply limited. The subject of the meeting largely predetermines the composition of the American delegation. Take for example the delegation to the Intelsat conferences. The delegation was put together in the Office of U.N. Political Affairs of the Bureau of International Organization Affairs. In assembling the delegation, the U.N. Office sought two qualities: (1) technical and legal knowledge, and (2) experience and contacts acquired from previous conferences. Constraints were the budget allotted and the need to maintain a low profile. Less prosperous nations resent the ease with which the United States can assemble a large number of technical and legal experts. The New York site for the meetings made it even easier than usual for the United States to overwhelm the other countries' delegations. Hence, to forestall any backlash, the U.N. Office took care to minimize the number of delegates present. Within the framework of these requirements and constraints, various agencies had to be represented. As a minimum State's International Organizations Bureau, NASA, and the Department of Defense had to be included. If legal issues were anticipated, State's Legal Bureau had to have a place. Likewise the Science Bureau demanded a place if technical issues were on the agenda. The FCC and the Economic Bureau required inclusion if the meeting touched on communications broadcasting. A private broadcaster from the educational television network requested membership on the delegation to one of the meetings. The U.N. Office declined to accredit him but invited him to attend as an observer. Once the sessions began, the technical knowledge of this NET official proved to be invaluable. Bernard Cohen relates a similar experience at the Tokyo negotiations for the North Pacific Fisheries Convention in 1951.[19] Japanese and Canadian opposition to the American proposed draft treaty necessitated complete rewriting. The only members of the American delegation with sufficient technical knowledge to participate in writing the new draft were the representatives of private fisheries associations who were originally included on the delegation merely to pacify West Coast political interests.

Although the State Department has the jurisdiction over assembling delegates to international meetings, its domain is not always respected fully. The Treasury frequently flouts the State Department's jurisdiction. The Treasury concedes that the State Department names the delegates to international meetings but it does not consider that international financial meetings come under that category. When such a meeting is held the Treasury determines who it will send without consulting State. Neither the Labor Department nor NASA act so independently. These two agencies defer to Foggy Bottom in assembling delegations.

A training program is a Group 2 commodity. It consists of an assembly of agency activities ordered in a way to best teach the trainee about his new job. Such on-the-job training programs represent a lower level of bureaucratic manufacturing than more formal classroom teaching. Still, the distinction is a matter of degree. There is no clear boundary where training stops and teaching begins.

The Labor Department offers the most extensive, or at least the longest, interagency training program. Annually the Foreign Service selects three or four young FSOs, usually with about five years in the service, who have applied for the labor attaché program. These future labor attachés go to the ILAB for ten months of training. During the first four to five months the FSOs learn about the Federal agencies concerned with labor—the bureaus of the department: Manpower, BLS, Wage and Hour; other agencies: the National Labor Relations Board, the Office of Economic Opportunity, the Civil Rights Commission, the Social Security Administration, and the Commerce Department. They also familiarize themselves with non-governmental organizations—the AFL-CIO, the UAW, the Chamber of Commerce. In recent years the trainees have gone on a field trip to New York City to visit local unions. Next the FSOs go to Harvard Business School for its thirteen week trade union program. Their classmates are workers sent by their unions. After Harvard the ILAB sends the FSOs to various unions for a two week internship. Sometime during their training period the trainees go to Capitol Hill to meet the Congressmen holding key positions on committees concerned with labor. By this time the trainees have received their overseas assignment. They spend their last month at the ILAB preparing themselves for this specific post.[20] Thus the labor attaché training program consists of assembling experiences from the federal government, private organizations, and universities. Almost none of the activities are designed for the trainees *per se*.

Exhibits are assembled on a grand scale much as the labor packet is on the small scale. An exhibit is built from Group 1 commodities, often from other agencies. Its ultimate presentation to the public at a foreign trade fair or library requires the combined efforts of several agencies. The ILAB has a special exhibit division in its Office of Country Programs. Typical themes are the history of the American labor movement, current trade union activities, and government programs to aid workers. Since the International Office of NASA does not have its own exhibits division the space agency's Office of Public Affairs supplies the facilities for this.

Group 3: Refined Commodities

The third group on the continuum consists of refined commodities. These commodities undergo a more extensive manufacturing process than the assembled commodities of group two. They are refined from Group 1 and Group 2 commodities much as gasoline is refined from crude oil. This is a big group encompassing much of what is generally considered the output of bureaucratic work.

Within this grouping of refined commodities the first major category is advice. Advice, as the term is used here, tends to be oral, flexible, specific, and solicited. It is transmitted over the telephone, in internal memorandums, and in face to face meetings. It does not imply a firm commitment or categorical statement from which the advisor cannot back down. It applies to a specific issue under consideration. It is usually given on demand. One bureaucrat calls another, explains the problem, and requests an opinion. Of course, unsolicited advice is an omnipresent bane in the life of every bureaucrat.

Advice may be either substantive or strategic. All substantive advice is technical insofar as it derives from jurisdiction related expertise. Just as the astrophysicist is a technician of space, likewise the FSO claims to be a technician of diplomacy. But following more conventional usage, the State Department gives political advice while the domestic agencies give technical advice. For example, in planning the bilateral program with India for the construction of an educational television system to be broadcast from a satellite, the State Department advises on the political feasibility while NASA advises on the technical feasibility. The department's India desk determines whether India can afford to build the network, can agree on a language for broadcasting, and can carry through on a long range commitment. NASA determines whether the satellite can be built, whether the community receivers can pick up the signal and how long the satellite will live. Another example of State Department advice to NASA is expository. The Russian desk explains the workings of the Soviet government and the Academy of Science of the U.S.S.R. to aid NASA in proposing or executing an exchange of information such as the joint project on space bio-medicine.[21] The State Department is not the exclusive source of political advice. As the domestic agencies gain experience in international affairs they develop their own body of expertise so that they are able to manufacture political advice of their own. Within the domestic departments the bureau specializing in international affairs naturally becomes the best source of political advice. Within the limits of its manpower the Treasury's International Affairs branch rivals the State Department as a locus of advice-generating expertise. The International Affairs branch has been involved in international finance since long before the Second World War. Many of the senior staff have been monetary diplomats for decades. To a lesser extent the ILAB is able to offer political advice. Although the ILAB's birthdate as an individual bureau was 1962, the Labor Department has been involved with an international program since the end of World War II. Like the Treasury's International Office, the ILAB is staffed by men with years of diplomatic experience. NASA, being a new agency, does not have an equivalent repository of political expertise, but it is acquiring more of it each year.

The State Department offers more than just political advice. It has many technical experts within its walls. Economists make up the largest group. They are numerous and well trained. Yet because they are spread thin, their impact is diluted. State Department personnel policy also decreases their effectiveness. The rotation policy hinders building up skills. They are rotated from Washington to the field and from economic to political duties. Having less chance to develop expertise, they are less able to produce advice.

The State Department includes a corps of labor experts in some ways comparable to its economists, but smaller in number. In the field these labor experts are in the attaché positions. In Washington they are assigned as geographic bureau labor advisors or on the staff of the Office of Labor Affairs, which serves both the regular State Department and AID. The labor experts are less successful than the economists in generating technical advice for two reasons. First, they are few in number. In all of Foggy Bottom there are only about two dozen. Secondly, those in the Labor Office are not the technical labor experts; they are the political labor experts. Their job is to insure good liaison with the AFL-CIO and to stand up for the labor position in department meetings. The technical experts are the labor economists and statisticians down in Federal Triangle. The State Department labor "experts" cannot really generate expert advice.

Within the Labor Department the most sought after source of advice on specific problems is the Office of Country Programs. This office includes the geographic area specialists who follow the particular problems within their regions. These are the men who can best predict the consequences of a proposed program or the impact of a changed policy. They best can apply the more generalized statistics of the BLS or the programs of the Manpower Administration to an individual country.

Treasury expertise centers in three fields: finance, tax, and customs. The State Department competes, using its own staff, in all three areas. Of the three it does best in finance. It devotes relatively more manpower to it primarily because it feels the issues are more important than tax or customs. The Treasury has the advantage of devoting full time to finance, while in comparison, the State Department tends to dabble. In the tax field the Internal Revenue Service dominates. The State Department economists foray into the tax advice field only to recommend countries for which they would like the IRS to design a double taxation treaty. Even in the treaty's negotiations the diplomats defer to the IRS experts. In customs affairs the Bureau of Customs similarly dominates. The State Department only enters in a peripheral way.

Thus far the advice considered has been substantive. This is certainly the most prevalent kind. A second kind of advice traded between agencies is strategic. It is procedural; it tells how to win the bureaucratic game. Most of this sort of advice is given within the confines of a single agency. It carries a stigma of intrigue and immorality. Yet not all is exchanged in whispered tones within the brotherhood. Occasionally strategic advice is conveyed to other agencies and even to people outside the federal government. Indeed the Science Bureau of the State Department devotes a large portion of its time to advising private companies. The Science Bureau is one of several agencies which must approve licenses for exports falling under the provisions of the Munitions Control Act. The Science Bureau is willing to review a company's application informally before it is submitted. A potential exporter can receive guidance enabling him to be sure his business deal will go through without difficulty. One FSO interviewed said that the companies cooperate readily in making revisions to comply with the provisions of the Act. They seem quite grateful for the department's advice on how to behave. With some dismay he added, "these companies come in here with the craziest ideas."

Agencies often advise on the strategy for getting a law they want from a recalcitrant Congress or how to secure the concurrence of a third agency with an interest in the program. The offices of congressional relations found in all departments testify to the high degree of importance attached to congressional strategy. These offices specialize in the "care and feeding" of congressional committee chairmen. In interagency dealings the Treasury's International Affairs branch prides itself on its superior knowledge of congressional behavior. The Treasury believes that it can advise on strategy better because lower personnel turnover leaves a larger residue of experience and because Congress and the Treasury share similar attitudes of fiscal conservatism not held by other agencies. The Treasury knows, for example, that Congress will not approve of one of the international banking institutions making a loan to a country which has recently expropriated American owned property. When the State Department insists on such a loan despite Treasury warnings, the Treasury will have State put its position in writing in a letter or memorandum so that it may absolve itself of the blame when Congress disapproves the transaction.

Advice may be rendered in unexpected forms. Several Treasury officials interviewed said that they occasionally had to advise State Department personnel that the positions they (the State Department personnel) were putting forward were not in accord with regular State Department policy. These inexperienced personnel did not know the position of their own department. The Treasury men would correct them even when State's policy disagreed with their own because they realized that any agreements reached on this basis would have to be revised when the error was discovered. Donald R. Mathews has noted a similar pattern of the veteran advising the novice in the policy position he should take even though this position was against the veteran's own interests.[22] Senior legislators advised freshmen how to vote in terms of the freshmen's constituencies. Francis E. Rourke points out a similar anomaly with the political appointee and the career civil servant.[23] The appointee is supposed to know politics; and the careerist, to know the technical subject. But in fact the appointee is often politically inexperienced and needs the advice of the careerist who has been preparing for congressional hearings for years, and the appointee is often more of an expert in his technical field than the civil servant.

John Harr offers a possible explanation for the inexperience of the State Department official. He notes that the main career path for FSOs is the political. Those who deviate from the mainstream into specialized areas of economics tend to be the more marginal officers who are less socialized by and less aware of the Department's policy and mores.[24] These are the personnel with whom the Treasury deals on financial questions.

In bureaucratic strategy, just as in military, good intelligence of the opponent is required. To the G-2, order of battle means the identity, strength, and disposition of the enemy units. Bureaucratic strategists, too, seek to learn the other agency's order of battle—who supports and who opposes their proposal, what influence each has, where they are located, what their capabilities and inclinations are. Bureaucratic allies occasionally exchange order of battle information. This information helps in planning a strategy to gain support. The amount of order of battle information offered in exchange varies according to the solidarity of the cross-agency alliance. If the alliance is long-standing, an agency can convey more order of battle information with the confidence that its distribution will be limited. If the alliance is temporary, an agency will be more circumspect since it faces the danger of exposure.

The second major category of commodities within the refined group complements those categorized as advice. The best generic term seems to be "papers." Whereas advice tended to be oral, flexible, specific, and solicited; papers tend to be written, firm, general, and unsolicited. Papers include reports, position papers, draft congressional testimony, and publications. They represent firm, considered opinions hammered out by interagency drafting groups after extensive discussion and debate. Papers are written for general rather than specific application. The time of their appearance depends on a schedule or upon the completion of the work, rather than the imperatives of a particular question.

Reports for the embassies are the least formal of the papers considered here. The reports cover areas such as the political or economic situation in a country. They are prepared cooperatively by the members of the embassy country team concerned with an area. The staff gathers information, analyzes it, and comments on its significance. This is an archetype of the refined commodity. The embassy staff takes commodities like information of the Group 1 type and from them "manufactures" a Group 3 commodity. The regular reports go back to the desk officer in the geographic bureau in Washington. He forwards photostats of various sections to other bureaucrats and other agencies as appropriate. In addition, an attaché will file special reports for the domestic agency whose interests he represents. The labor attaché sends a quarterly report on the labor situation. The ILAB supplies him with the forms which he fills in. As appropriate, he writes special reports on events such as a strike or unemployment or a visit by American trade unionists. Besides keeping tabs on local unions, the labor attaché observes any exports to the United States which might affect American workers. The Labor Department maintains a sharp lookout for any foreign production that might endanger the jobs of American workers. Among other things, the attaché checks that workers producing imports competing with American production are paid a fair (i.e., high) wage.

Since the sixteen Treasury representatives stationed abroad are not in the Foreign Service, they are more autonomous in reporting. They aid the FSO economic officer in preparing his report, but their own goes directly to the Treasury without being channeled through Foggy Bottom. NASA obtains little information via the Foreign Service science attachés. Most comes from the regular system of scientific publication.

Policy papers represent a higher degree of refinement than reports. Strictly speaking, the State Department distinguishes a number of different kinds of papers setting forth policy. A formal "policy paper" is long range and general. It covers U.S. policy toward a given country or region for as long as five, ten, or more years. Many bureaus and agencies contribute. It requires extensive preparation and clearances. First, a working draft is hammered out in house (i.e., within the department). Next the State Department invites interested parties to an interagency meeting for further revisions. Finally a revised version is circulated for approval. The State Department jealously guards its prerogatives to prepare policy papers. Prior to 1969 the Policy Planning Council (PPC) was responsible for preparing these long range papers. Channels of access for input from the other agency were more formal and regular. The PPC demanded a steady stream of papers from the ILAB for the labor section of the total country policy papers. Since the abolition of the PPC, the five geographic bureaus each handle the policy papers of their own countries. The procedure is more ad hoc. The ILAB officials interviewed prefer the old system. They believe that by submitting formal papers to the PPC they enjoyed greater influence than in the present system of offering informal suggestions to the geographic bureaus.

When the White House wanted to define the American policy on the use of direct broadcast satellites it assigned the responsibility for supervision to the Office of Telecommunication Policy in the Executive Office of the President. The State Department objected that it was the exclusive foreign policy making agency in the U.S. government. The Office of Telecommunication Policy was not authorized to make foreign policy. Accordingly, the Telecommunication Office changed the name of its project to a "staff study paper."

The State Department calls papers prepared to instruct a delegation to an international meeting position papers. These are prepared in a fashion similar to that used for policy papers: first, in house discussion, then interagency meetings, and finally revision and clearances. Other papers of the same type are those prepared at the request of the White House or the Secretary of State.

A speech is a version of a policy statement. Although delivered orally, it is basically a policy paper in terms of its preparation and importance. All the bureaus have some demand for speech writing. Some have a high demand. The U.N. Office is constantly writing statements for the American representatives to the General Assembly, the Security Council, and the committees. Another bureau in the department had few occasions requiring speeches, but one man on its staff had earned a reputation for his skill as a ghost writer. High officials from his own department, other departments, and even the president have called on him for speech texts. One of the speech commodities most in demand is testimony for congressional committee hearings.[25] This includes both testimony to be delivered orally and statements to be inserted into the record. The agencies understand well the importance of these presentations and prepare extensively.

Policy papers are a double edged commodity. On one side the input commodity is words, on the other, it is ideas. In actuality it is both. To say that it is only ideas is unsatisfactory because the agencies spend hours arguing over specific wording. For centuries politicians and diplomats have appreciated the importance of the smallest variations in wording. But the words are argued over only because of the ideas behind them. Whether a word is removed or retained can mean an agency's position is rejected or accepted. The bureaucrats who live by these policy papers are intelligent men trained to appreciate subtle distinctions in wording.

Publications are the most firm and general papers produced by the bureaucracy. They range from congressional testimony, which is a transitional form, being a policy paper which finds its way into print, to technical publications of the Bureau of Labor Statistics. The BLS is the most demanded bureaucratic producer. It is a factory which manufactures statistics and reports from the raw information it consumes. It produces the series on Labor Law and Practice. Other series cover labor developments and situations around the world. It produces manuals for AID such as "How to Make an Inventory of High Level and Skilled Manpower in Developing Countries." The BLS follows Eastern Europe closely. This contrasts with the ILAB policy of ignoring the Communist-bloc countries for ideological reasons. There are no labor attachés in Communist countries because the AFL-CIO vetoes dealing with trade unions that are government controlled. Since the ILAB is not interested in BLS output on Eastern Europe, one possibility is that this commodity is produced for the Central Intelligence Agency. Another possibility is that the Labor Department is really interested in the Eastern European labor situation but places responsibility for analysis in the BLS because it is less exposed to criticism than the more visible ILAB. The ILAB publishes its own monographs in the International Labor Studies series. Representative titles include *The Miners International Federation* and *The International Metal Workers Federation.*

The Treasury produces statistics in much the same way as the BLS, albeit on a smaller scale. Using figures gathered by its own foreign representatives, by the Foreign Service economic officers, and by the Department of Commerce, it manufactures statistics. The Treasury takes the raw data from abroad, refines it, and produces a balance sheet of the national financial position. This balance of payments in turn is useful to other agencies including those which helped collect the raw data originally.

Publicity is a commodity often traded in the foreign policy arena. The ILAB and the International Office of NASA have their own public affairs personnel. The Treasury's International Affairs branch depends on personnel in the Office of Public Affairs. These "information specialists," as they modestly call themselves, crank out hundreds of press releases in the course of a year. Regular news media pick up some of the stories, but most go to specialized publications such as trade union newspapers, aviation magazines, and financial journals. When a news item is prepared in house as a press release, the production is within the bureaucracy. But when a news reporter gathers the information and writes his own story he is the manufacturer. In a typical news interview both the agency official and the reporter generate a refined commodity. The official seldom is satisfied with conveying plain information. He puts in his own analysis of the situation, or rather he puts in the agency's official position. The reporter takes this already refined information from the official spokesman and further refines it.

The commodity which epitomizes the State Department's mission is international negotiation. The Foreign Service corps prides itself on producing this most diplomatic of all the commodities. Negotiation is placed in Group 3 because it is a highly refined product characterized by planning, analysis, and internal consensus building comparable to that displayed in writing a policy paper. Indeed, for complex negotiations, writing a position paper is a preliminary step to the actual discussion with the foreign negotiators.

The State Department has negotiated numerous treaties and agreements for NASA. Many of these were for tracking and communication ground stations. When the space agency first recognizes the need for a new tracking station in a foreign country it goes to the State Department. The State Department has the embassy arrange for a team of NASA technicians to survey possible sites. Once the technicians find a suitable site the embassy negotiates a bilateral agreement on the specifics. The usual form is the exchange of notes between the American ambassador and the foreign minister. The agreement identifies the site, provides the funding, personnel and access policies, and assures the site will be protected from radio interference. The host country names one of its own government bureaus as a "Cooperating Agency" to work directly with NASA on more detailed arrangements.

The U.S.-Japan agreement on space cooperation is another product of bilateral negotiations.[26] By 1967 the embassy in Tokyo realized that the Japanese planned to move into space regardless of whether the United States aided them or not. Ambassador U. Alexis Johnson decided that it would be best to cooperate, since not cooperating would do little to deter them. The embassy initiated negotiations on the terms of this cooperation. The American negotiators sought three conditions. First was the peaceful use of space. The Japanese readily agreed to that. Second was that technology from the United States was not to go to a third country without American permission. This was harder. The Japanese could not guarantee to keep the technology secret. Japanese laws against espionage are lax. Instead of law they rely on the private sanctions of loss of status within their strict social system to guard against technical espionage. The Japanese finally were able to provide guarantees sufficient to satisfy the Americans. The third goal of the American negotiators was that the Japanese not use the technology to infringe on Intelsat. The State Department is committed to a single global communication system. In other words, it insists on an American monopoly. NASA is less committed to Intelsat. After eighteen months of negotiations all interested parties were satisfied, NASA as well as the Japanese, and the treaty was signed.

Multilateral treaties are harder to negotiate than bilateral ones. The Treaty on the Exploration and Use of Outer Space was the first multilateral space agreement. It was drawn up under the auspices of the U.N. Committee on the Peaceful Uses of Outer Space. Negotiations were completed, the draft approved by the U.N. Committee and the treaty was opened for signature on January 27, 1967. Negotiations proceeded fairly rapidly. One reason was that the Space Treaty was based on the Antarctic Treaty of 1960. Another reason was that issues in contention between the United States and U.S.S.R. were simply omitted.[27]

The Space Treaty of 1967 was soon followed by the Agreement on the Rescue and Return of Astronauts.[28] Bin Cheng has criticized this agreement in the 1969 *Year Book of World Affairs*.[29] Cheng charges that the negotiators were so concerned with speed that they produced a sloppy and empty treaty. He asserts that the Rescue Agreement provides little of substance because the nations of the world had no intention of keeping any astronauts or spacecraft which fell into their territory. Those benefits which are provided accrue entirely to the big space powers, not the small nations which really need a liability treaty protecting them from space junk landing on top of them.

The negotiations the State Department conducts for the Treasury lack the glamorous subject matter of negotiations for NASA. At the same time their impact is far greater. In defense of the America's precarious balance of payments situation the State Department has negotiated a series of agreements with European countries. Currently the State Department is negotiating military offset arrangements. The United States wants the Europeans to contribute to the cost of maintaining American troops for NATO defense. The Department of Defense gathers data on the balance of payments deficit costs of maintaining the troops. The Treasury analyzes (or as one interviewee said, "massages") the data to produce some meaningful statistics and the State Department uses these statistics in its negotiations. Treasury officials believe that the State Department is advancing its own interests in the process. They claim that the State Department has taken the lead in negotiating military offset arrangements because they do not want to bring the troops home and a military offset will convince Congress that it can afford to keep the troops in Europe.

Image is a commodity best categorized in Group 3. Like the other commodities in this group it is a highly refined product of bureaucratic manufacturing. It is a more ephemeral output than advice or policy papers or even negotiations. Although there is no theoretical restriction on it, those interviewed mentioned image only in connection with one of the four agencies. And remarkably they mentioned this agency both as a consumer and a producer of image. Which agency that is should come as no surprise; it is NASA.

NASA produces a good image by being peaceful, scientific, generous, daring, and winning. Its mission is non-military, thanks to the U.S. Air Force handling the military aspects of space. It has a completely open devotion to gaining and sharing scientific information. It shares some of the glory as well as the information with tokens like carrying miniature flags of all nations to the moon. Its exploration captures the world's craving for adventure. And finally, in recent years at least, it has "defeated" Russia in the unadmitted space race. This is NASA as a manufacturer of image. But NASA is helped in the business of image production by the State Department, in particular the International Organizations Bureau and the USIA. The U.N. Office of the International Organizations Bureau describes the U.N. Committee on the Peaceful Uses of Outer Space as a "projection point for NASA's image." The U.N. Office projects a favorable view of NASA's operations before this body. It also advises NASA on how to do things that will please the committee. The USIA's "projection point" for NASA's image is world wide. USIS movies, press releases, moon rock displays, etc., all help manufacture the good image.

Political support is a commodity eagerly sought by agencies. Most agencies think of themselves so much as consumers that they fail to recognize that they are also producers of this commodity. One feature of political support is that it tends to be produced at a different level than that at which it is consumed. A particular bureau may get political support from above itself in the hierarchy (the department secretary) or from below (a clientele group). In turn the secretary may get political support from that bureau in the form of rank and file enthusiasm for a policy.

Political support is produced either internally or externally to the executive branch. The best quality of internal support is that coming from the president. One interviewee stated that his department used the president's policy declarations as a "weapon" in interagency negotiations. Second best is support from the secretary of the department. Another interviewee said that the fastest way to win a point in his department is to be able to say "this is the way the secretary wants it." He calls this "the invoking of names," and proudly claimed that "we use it whenever possible." When an agency is unable to invoke the names of superiors it must fall back on the political support which it produces at its own level. This usually takes the negative form of cutting off the exchange of commodities with the other agency. The agency will threaten not to cooperate in the future. In extreme cases an agency will threaten to lobby against the other agency.

The State Department and its constituent bureaus tend to be more prone to dealing in internally produced political support than the domestic agencies which deal more in externally produced support. One reason is that the State Department does not have much external support. What political support it does have is produced internally. Secondly, in the past state has had a tradition of close ties to the president. Presidential support is the best kind. Thirdly, lacking a subject matter base, the State Department is more oriented toward hierarchy. Invoking names carries more weight in the State Department than it does in the domestic departments where subject matter related expertise is more important. The USIA, for example, has no mission other than propagating the party line, or as one spokesman phrased it: "to support U.S. foreign policy as enunciated by the White House and the State Department." To keep the USIA straight Foggy Bottom sends it daily foreign policy guidance. The other State Department bureaus do not display quite as much willingness to follow the official doctrine, but approach the issue with more autonomy. The Science Bureau describes its job as filling in the lacunae of foreign policy when it touches on science: How do scientific programs conform to the foreign policy enunciated from above. The International Organizations Bureau, like the USIA, is concerned with projecting the official American foreign policy, in this case before the United Nations. Of course the various bureaus do not follow the official doctrine slavishly. There is much give and take, up and down the hierarchy. Still, the State Department bureaus are more prone to value highly political support produced at a higher level than are the domestic departments.

The domestic departments are able to obtain political support from outside the bureaucracy. Clientele groups are the best sources. Trade union support of the Labor Department is a classic example. This commodity is delivered in the form of testimony before Congress committees, lobbying on the Hill, and telephone calls to the president. NASA gets external political support from the aerospace industry and, more than the other departments, from the general public which applauds the American venture into space. The Treasury draws support from bankers, businessmen, and all others who favor conservative fiscal policies. Political support from the legislative and the judicial branches of the federal government are forms of external support. Firm backing of a congressional committee is an invaluable commodity. Although the courts rarely enter the picture, their intervention can best be categorized here.

In practice the commodity of political support is not quite as straightforward as this. While the State Department as a whole may lack a general clientele, its individual bureaus often have clienteles. The Economic Bureau enjoys the active support of businesses engaged in foreign trade. The Science Bureau has a strong clientele in the aerospace industry. AID in past years enjoyed the favor of the trade unions. George Meany used to testify in its behalf at congressional appropriations hearings. On the other hand, the domestic agencies do not always enjoy effective political support from their clientele. The Treasury in particular feels that its clientele does not carry much weight with congressmen because of their old populist suspicion of bankers.

Group 4: Invented Commodities

The fourth and final group on the continuum consists of new commodities invented by the agencies. These are commodities which never existed before. They are equivalent to new inventions in industry or the discovery of new knowledge in science. This group includes preparations for an unknown future. Contingency planning is one form. Spontaneous inventions and initial international meetings are others. Invented commodities differ from refined commodities insofar as they are original creations. These commodities are invented to cope with a problem the first time it occurs. Once routinized, they are considered in Group 3 or even Group 1 or 2 as appropriate. Like the refined commodities of Group 3, Group 4 commodities are produced from other commodities from Groups 1 and 2.

One bureaucratic invention is the DISC.[30] DISC is the acronym for Domestic-International Sales Corporation. The Treasury invented the DISC as a device for stimulating exports. Most European countries give tax deferment to exporters in order to make their products more competitive in the world market. The United States is prohibited by the General Agreement on Tariffs and Trade (GATT) from giving a similar deferment to American exporters because of its different tax structure. The Europeans tax value added whereas the United States taxes corporate income. GATT allows a deferment for a tax on value added but not for income tax. To circumvent this GATT provision the Treasury has proposed the DISC. Any American corporation wishing to recieve a tax deferment on exports would incorporate a DISC subsidiary. The DISC would export for the parent corporation and would be eligible to receive the tax deferment. For many years the United States has offered a similar deferment for investment abroad. The DISC was invented by the Treasury, more exactly by the Internal Revenue Service. The Treasury "sold" it to the other agencies concerned. They in turn suggested some modifications. The Treasury wanted to describe it as a "subsidy" to gain business support but the State Department cautioned it that "subsidies" are a violation of the GATT. A tax deferment is not. The DISC proposal was quickly accepted within the bureaucracy, where everyone was pro-export, and was sent to Congress as part of the 1970 trade bill.

The earth resources survey (ERS) is another example of an invented commodity.[31] NASA developed the ERS as a way to extend the benefits of the space programs to the underdeveloped nations which form, in effect, a clientele group of the State Department. The ERS is a system of photographing the earth from a satellite. These photographs can be used to monitor crops, identify plant diseases, prepare maps, and evaluate hydrographic and mineral resources. When NASA proposed its invention it was overwhelmed with the enthusiastic response of the underdeveloped nations. These nations overestimated the speed with which the satellite would be ready. NASA does not plan to have it operational until 1972. It is still too early to set up training programs for application of the ERS. Training technicians prematurely would only lead to frustration and disillusionment.

To meet the demands of the underdeveloped nations generated by the promise of the ERS, NASA had to invent another commodity. The underdeveloped nations had proposed a major ERS conference under United Nations auspices. NASA feared that a conference of this type would be scientifically unproductive and would produce pressure on them to give a higher priority to the program. NASA proposed a more technically oriented conference as an alternative. Its International Office made all the arrangements for this conference held in Vienna in the spring of 1970.[32] Besides taking the pressure off NASA, the Vienna conference produced some worthwhile scientific results. First, the participants learned that there already was a great store of information on earth resources. Many of the techniques of satellite photography are adaptable to aerial photography. Secondly, the underdeveloped nations set up cooper-

ative panels of technicians. This reduced the number of personnel these countries wished to train to a smaller and more manageable size. Thirdly, international workshops on the ERS were planned for the spring of 1971.

In the invented commodities considered thus far the invention has either been
spontaneous, such as the DISC, or has arisen as the result of the invention, such
as the underdeveloped nations demands of the ERS applications. In these cases
the problem and the solutions come on the scene together. The invented commodity structures its own future. But in foreign affairs it is probably more
common to have a problem with no solution. One of the major functions of the
agencies in the foreign affairs arena is to prepare for an unknown future. This
may involve contingency planning for disaster, structuring a fluid situation, or
merely projecting the present situation a little farther into the future.

The Science Bureau specializes in coping with disaster. Apollo 13 provided
ample opportunity. First, the bureau faced up to the possibility that the astronauts might not return safely to earth. It prepared two messages thanking the
nations of the world for their offers to help in recovery—one if the astronauts
returned and another if they did not. Happily, the first was sent. Second, the
bureau realized that Apollo 13 was bringing home some unwanted baggage. The
lunar module carried the SNAP-27 containing 8.5 pounds of radioactive plutonium. The SNAP-27 was a nuclear power package scheduled to remain on the
lunar surface to generate electricity for experiments set up by the astronauts.
Because of its density the plutonium would not burn up with the rest of the
lunar module as it fell through the atmosphere on reentry but would plummet
down to the earth's surface. The Bureau had the job of guarding against scientific backlash. Fortunately for the State Department backlash never developed
for when the lunar module reentered, the plutonium fell harmlessly into the
Pacific Ocean and is thought to lie now in a watery grave at the bottom of the
Tonga Trench northeast of New Zealand.

The space program has created other problems of preparing for an unknown
future that are less sensational than Apollo 13 but equally complex. The immi-
nent emergence of satellites capable of broadcasting television directly to individual receivers threatens the integrity of every national culture. At worst it is
the spectre of space propagandists broadcasting to an eager audience of impres-
sionable television viewers.[33] The lesser threat is that of cultural imperialism.
The English and Russian languages will predominate. People will watch cowboy
movies to the neglect of their own national heritages. To guarantee against this
apparition of the future the United Nations established the Direct Broadcasting
Working Group. This Working Group is charged with structuring a system of
control over direct broadcasting that will protect national sovereignty. The development of communication satellites in the mid-1960s presented a similar
problem. The existing system of transoceanic communication had been developed contractually by private cable owners over the course of the previous
century. When satellite communication threatened to revolutionize the system,

the cable companies sought government intervention. The threat of the unknown exceeded their fears of governmental control.

The Treasury's clientele group of international bankers can no more tolerate an unknown future than the cable owners can. Like the cable owners, the bankers turn to the government for security. The bankers want to guarantee that the system of fixed exchange rates will continue as smoothly as possible into the future. They fear an unpredictable foreign currency market. They perceive their market threatened by speculators, or as they quaintly refer to them, the gnomes of Zurich.[34] The bankers do not seem willing to accept a free market. The theoretical function of a bank is to accept short term deposits and invest them as long term. There is a built-in tension in this because the short term and the long term are not always compatible. The bankers are not willing to accept managing this tension as part of their responsibility so they demand that the Treasury eliminate the tension by stabilizing the exchange ratios between currencies. Since 1944 the system of fixed exchange rates has done this, but the flaw with the system is the danger of devaluation. Therefore, the bankers want the Treasury to work to counter speculation against a weak currency. The U.S. Treasury, along with the other IMF treasuries, does this, but when the cost goes too high, as in 1967 for the pound sterling or 1971 for the dollar, they abandon their efforts and over a weekend the currency drops sharply in value, much to the consternation of the bankers.

The four agencies vary in their propensity to invent commodities. NASA and the State Department are more inventive than the Treasury and the Labor Department. This is in keeping with the overall characteristics of the four agencies. NASA is intended to be technologically innovative. This carries over into its international affairs. The State Department has a role of planning rather than performance. To maintain its purity it has spawned two semi-autonomous agencies to do the work: USIA and AID. The Labor Department and the Treasury are basically performing agencies. They do the work as well as the thinking. And of course, to a lesser extent, they do invent commodities themselves. There is a pattern of a commodity shifting from one agency to another as it shifts from Group 4 to Group 3. That is, a commodity invented in one agency shifts to another when its production becomes routine. The Early Bird communication satellite was initially developed by NASA in the early 1960s. When communication satellites became operational in 1965 NASA relinquished control to the FCC and the Comsat Corporation. NASA is now developing the ERS program. When it becomes effective the Agency plans to transfer it to the Department of the Interior. NASA is beginning to experiment with television broadcasting from a satellite. It does not intend to operate a television network in the future but to transfer it to the FCC or some agency yet to be created. The State Department invented the Marshall Plan in 1948 but, like NASA, saw its role as innovation rather than performance and so created the ECA, now AID, to run the program. One reason the State Department avoids performance is that it lacks resources. It has a low budget and few facilities. It can no longer even afford to pay travel expenses, as it did in the past, of officials from other departments who are members of official delegations to international meetings. Now their own agency must pay for them.

This discussion of invented commodities concludes the long survey of the commodities of bureaucratic exchange. It began with the transmitted commodities in Group 1 whose form remained unchanged, including the institutionalized controls over the flow of other commodities in votes and vetoes, licenses and credentials, and guarantees of professional standards as well as the more conventional goods, services, raw information, personnel, and money. Next were the assembled commodities of Group 2: the assembled information, visits and trips, training programs, and exhibits. After this came the refined commodities of Group 3. These included advice, papers, negotiations, image, and political support. Finally, Group 4 comprises the invented commodities discussed here.

Utility and Preference

Two agencies exchange commodities because both benefit. Each agency values the commodity of the other more highly than it values its own commodity which it is giving up. An exchange represents not an equality of two commodities but two inequalities of value.[1] Economists have traditionally used the term utility to describe the value one agency or one person attaches to a commodity.[2] It is subjective. It is the psychic worth of a commodity seen from the view point of a single agency or person, not the worth of that commodity to others or in the market place.

Utility has two components: taste and quantities possessed.[3] An agency's taste is a function of its goals. The Labor Department prefers commodities which help the American worker. NASA prefers commodities which advance space science. The Treasury prefers commodities which strengthen the economy; and the State Department, commodities which advance American foreign policy.[4] This is the picture in general. In its specifics the particular tastes of the agencies yield some more useful insights. For example, the Labor Department is officially committed to all labor, not just organized labor. The labor attachés are supposed to carry this attitude with them to their overseas assignments. On the job the attaché is supposed to be labor-conscious, not an advocate for trade unionism. But the labor attaché is often strongly committed to a pro-union ideology. Thus his preference for labor exceeds its official bounds. AID has a different source of a preference for fostering trade unionism. Its legislation charges it to develop democratic institutions. Free trade unions are one such institution.[5] An incidental benefit of a pro-union taste by the labor attachés and AID is that these unions are likely to raise wages, thereby making their exports less competitive with American production. The AFL-CIO prefers foreign aid programs which benefit the workers. These do not have to be specifically labor programs. Its taste is for assistance which helps the ordinary people.

NASA has a taste for the technical. It prefers commodities which help in accomplishing its mission. It values sites for tracking stations highly, something the Labor Department would value very low. Tracking stations are, in the opinions of one official interviewed, the space agency's first and most important foreign need. Not only does NASA have a preference for tracking stations, it has quite explicit preferences as to their exact locations. The sites must follow the launch pathway—from Cape Kennedy southeast along the Atlantic range, across South Africa, over Australia, and north across the Pacific over Hawaii. Stations out of tracking range have a low utility to NASA. NASA has a taste for openness. It values open access to technical information, to sites around the world, and to the radio frequencies. In turn NASA has developed an ideology of openness. It gives free access to its own information, sites, etc.

NASA's tastes run toward goals; the Treasury, on the other hand, prefers security. It is inconceivable that the Treasury would ever attach much utility to the freedom to experiment that NASA prizes so highly. Experimentation is the last thing these conservative financiers seek. They want a smooth running, predictable foreign currency market. They have no more use for experiments then they have for tracking stations. Nor do they attach much value to strengthening free labor unions abroad.

Those involved in the Intelsat Consortium share the Treasury's preference for a stable and predictable future. At the time communication satellites began to emerge as a commercial enterprise, their concern was for a prompt determination of the structure of the communication market. The cable companies preferred a quick decision to a "best" decision.[6] With the shift of the satellites from NASA to Comsat, there was a shift of utility from experimentation to practicality.

Not surprisingly, the State Department's tastes run toward the diplomatic. It values projects of other agencies that help it to advance U.S. foreign policy. The State Department cares little for NASA's scientific product but a great deal for its diplomatic, or to use the department's term, political, by-product. One FSO expressed both his gratitude for this by-product and his foreign policy orientation when he said: "We have to look at NASA's great gift to us from its political point of view." A second FSO expressed his preference for the political rather than the scientific contribution when he described the space program as "one of the most hopeful tools of international cooperation."

The preferences of the domestic agencies reflect the preferences of their clientele groups. The State Department has the equivalent of a clientele group in the foreign countries with which it conducts diplomacy. The State Department's tastes run toward serving the interests of these 127 nations. Indeed, the other agencies occasionally criticize Foggy Bottom for preferring the interests of these nations to the American national interest. "The State Department represents foreigners," they complain.

The second component of utility is the quantity possessed. This leads to the law of diminishing marginal utility which states that (after a certain point) each additional increment of a commodity added to one's stock will be less valued than the previous increment. Although total utility will be increased, the marginal utility will decrease with each additional unit. Thus one will be willing to offer to exchange some units of a commodity of which he is well supplied in return for some other commodity since the marginal utility of the former is less than the marginal utility of the latter.

Kenneth Boulding phrases this "the more of anything we have . . ., the less we want more of it.[7] And what one has the most of is that which one produces oneself. What one has least of is that which someone else produces. An agency puts a low utility on its own product because it has so much and a high utility on the product of other agencies because it has so little. Many a bureaucrat thinks his agency is doing all the getting and is giving very little in return. In the context of microeconomic theory this feeling of exploiting the other is natural because one places a low value on his own agency's output and a high value on that of the other agency. Both parties to an exchange typically express attitudes of receiving more than they are giving.[8] An FSO said "NASA has made a great contribution to American foreign policy." Another added, "Apollo is one of the greatest things helping us along in our foreign relations." At the other end of the Mall, a NASA official said, "The relationship is more one of NASA utilizing the State Department than vice versa."

The Agreement on the Rescue and Return of Astronauts demonstrates how utility may vary because of differing quantities possessed, even though tastes are identical. Both the United States and the U.S.S.R. have the same preference for the rescue and return of their astronauts and their space vehicles. But their accesses to the territories where they might land in an emergency diverge. The U.S.S.R. possesses a large quantity of access to territory in Communist bloc nations. The United States has access to the rest of the nations and the high seas. Thus the Russians have a large quantity of one commodity (access within the Communist bloc) and a small quantity of the other commodity (access to the rest of the globe). Since the United States possesses these commodities in the opposite proportion, their utilities are complementary and both can benefit by the exchange.

The utility of bureaucratic intelligence varies according to the quantity possessed. Each of the bureaus studied has a large quantity of intelligence about itself and a small quantity of intelligence about its counterpart. A number of officials interviewed said that in its search for intelligence information their own bureau was often quite willing, even eager, to reveal its secrets (on which it placed a low utility) in return for the scarce secrets of the other agency (on which it placed high utility).

In these last two examples the utilities of the parties to the exchange have been complementary, but this is not always the case. Agencies' utilities frequently diverge. The State Department's utility diverged from NASA's when Spain proposed to launch a series of sounding rockets.[9] Spanish scientists wanted to launch a sequence of experimental probes into the upper atmosphere from a Spanish range. NASA thought the project was trivial. The chief aim of the launch would be prestige rather than science. The State Department saw the political advantage in the scheme. Spain was host to a tracking station. It was the site of several military installations: a Navy base at Rota and an Air Force base near Madrid. Negotiations were then underway for the renewal of the treaty covering these bases. The utilities of the two agencies were not opposed but only divergent. The rocket launches were of some utility to NASA but, at first, not of high enough utility to make the project worthwhile. Their utility to the State Department was high enough. Finally the State Department was able to increase the utility to NASA enough to persuade them to launch the rockets for Spain.

NASA and the State Department had a similar divergence of utility in a Brazilian request to study coffee rust.[10] Brazil wanted NASA to survey the extent this disease had damaged their coffee crop using remote sensing equipment in high flying aircraft. NASA was reluctant to commit its limited resources to this survey. The State Department, whose utility was political rather than scientific, thought the project worthwhile and in the end persuaded NASA to fly the missions.

The differing orientation of utility between the State Department and NASA does not automatically mean that the State Department favors cooperative projects and NASA does not. Their respective political versus scientific utilities may put them in the reverse situation. In 1967 India and the United States undertook an experimental project to broadcast educational television programs directly from a satellite to community receivers. NASA was enthusiastic, while the India desk at the State Department was not. The political utility was low even though the scientific utility was high. Willis H. Shapley, Associate Deputy Administrator of NASA, referred to this pattern of high scientific utility and low political utility in testimony to the Senate Aeronautics and Space Science Committee. Referring to cooperative projects with the U.S.S.R. he said, "I am sure that from a scientist to scientist standpoint, there is a much greater urge for meaningful cooperation than there is at the political level."[11]

In the labor field utilities diverge along domestic versus foreign considerations. The Labor Department's utility is based on the welfare of the American workers as they are affected by labor events abroad. One part, but only one part, of the American worker's concern with foreign labor is an ideological dedication to promotion of a democratic labor movement in these countries. A second part of the workers' concern stems from fear of competition with cheap foreign labor. Even within the State Department, the utilities of the component bureaus vary. AID has, as part of its legislative charter, the mission of fostering the development of democratic institutions, among them, free trade unions. The geographic bureaus, on the other hand, are generally interested only in the political importance of trade union activities.

Utility can vary according to the individual as well as according to the agency. The embassies devote a good deal of time and effort arranging for visitors from Washington. They are Uncle Sam's travel agency for high officials from the domestic agencies. But the value of this service varies sharply according to the utility of the individual traveler. Some want to be cloaked by the embassy, to have accommodations, appointments, and parties arranged for them. Others could not care less. The utility of the service is subjective.

Utilities do not necessarily diverge along obvious lines. Sometimes agencies or organizations will find their utilities to be coincident on an issue despite an overall divergence. Notwithstanding their differing orientations, NASA and the State Department agree that foreign astronauts should be integrated into the manned space program during the 1970s.[12] The State Department favors this because it would enhance America's image of seeking to use space peacefully for the benefit of all mankind. NASA favors it because it would increase the pool of talent on which to draw. Both agencies foresee foreign astronauts helping to man the permanent space station scheduled to be orbiting the earth by the late 1970s.[13] The space station would accommodate fifty to sixty astronaut-scientists who would conduct their experiment over a period of several months.

In spite of their frequent conflicts domestically, the utilities of labor and management often coincide on international issues. Within the textile industry both fear the increasing influx of Japanese imports. Concern with Japanese competition runs high at the ILAB. To help stem the tide the bureau created a new post of Deputy Assistant Secretary of Labor for Trade and Adjustment Policy.[14]

Since the concept of utility was developed in the nineteenth century, its critics have attacked it as being both incalculable and unnecessary. To eliminate the need for the concept, economists developed indifference curve analysis. Indifference curve analysis is based on the assumption that an economic actor is willing to trade off between his objectives. He will take less of one commodity if he can get more of another. There is a set of combinations of commodities which are equally acceptable to him, or to use the economic term, between which he is indifferent. Above it in desirability is another set of combinations, all of which are more desirable than the first set. Below it is a third set of combinations, none of which are as desirable as the first set. When the preferences of the actor are mapped, they form a series of curves. Each curve represents all combinations which are equally desirable. Moving northeast on the map each curve is more desirable than the preceding one. The actor wishing to improve his position strives to move northeast to progressively more desirable curves.[15]

Indifference curve analysis lends itself conveniently to explaining certain bureaucratic decisions in foreign policy because the issues tend to dichotomize into political versus technical functions. Decisions on space exploration divide roughly into political versus scientific dimensions. Decisions on labor affairs divide into political versus practical dimensions; those of finance, into political versus monetary.

Site selection is the best application. Vehicles launched into deep space demand a different network of tracking and communication facilities than do the earth orbiting satellites.[16] Since the stations must track and communicate with vehicles over the vast distances of space their broadcasts must be more powerful and their reception must be more sensitive. Since the spacecraft are farther from earth, they require fewer stations to track them. Three stations located 120 degrees apart around the earth, are sufficient to maintain contact twenty-four hours a day. The stations must be just outside the vehicle's path as projected on the earth. Since the path is approximately between 30 degrees north and 30 degrees south latitude, the tracking stations must be just north or just south of this belt. Moving a station too far north or south away from the belt makes tracking and communication more difficult. When NASA began to establish its deep space tracking network it already had one site at Goldstone, California. This dictated that the second site be 120 degrees to the east and just north or south of the 30 degrees latitude belt. This gave two "boxes" of possible sites, one in the western Mediterranean and the other in southern Africa. That was the technical dimension. The other was the political. Not all of the dozen or so countries that fell within these two geographical boxes were equally acceptable. Figure 3-1 is a graph of the indifference curves representing a theoretical re-

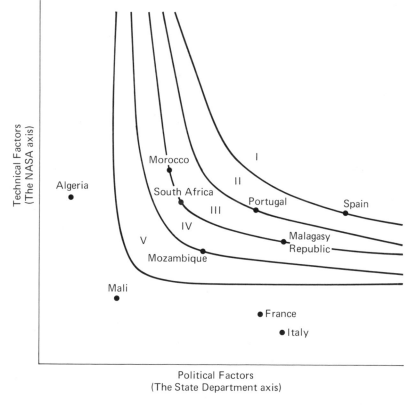

Figure 3-1.

capitulation of the decision-making process which culminated with the selection of the Madrid site. NASA officials did not actually draw such an indifference map, but when shown this map they acknowledged that it approximated the factors they considered in selecting the Madrid tracking site.

The dozen possible sites are placed on the map along political and technical axes. The political dimension refers to the willingness of the host to accept and support the site and the estimate of their continued support over the next ten to twenty years. A country presently desirable for a site might not be so if political instability led to hostility toward the American space program at some time in the future. The technical dimension refers to a geographical location, freedom from radio interference, surface communication facilities, transportation, a pool of competent local technicians, etc. To simplify, the map shows only one site per country. Actually a number of potential sites existed in each country. Thus the two axes—technical versus political—approximate the respective orientations of the two departments—NASA versus State—involved in the site selection process.

Spain, the country finally chosen, is shown on indifference curve I. This is the curve farthest to the northeast on the indifference map. Three countries, Morocco, the Union of South Africa, and the Malagasy Republic, appear on curve III. This indicates that these three countries were equally acceptable. NASA was indifferent between them. Curve V represents the absolute minimum of acceptability. Any country falling to the left of curve V is politically unacceptable. NASA thus eliminated Algeria even though it was technically satisfactory. Any country falling below curve V was technically unacceptable. NASA eliminated France and Italy for being outside the geographical box and Botswana because of its isolation and the low level of technical support it could provide. Mali was eliminated for both political and technical reasons. The graph shows that Spain lacked some technical characteristics. It was farther north than Morocco, almost at the northern limit of the box. But it compensated for this with better political conditions. It was this combination that put it on a higher indifference curve.

A third of the way around the world NASA looked for a site for its western station. Of the countries which fell into one of the two geographical boxes, Japan was the best choice politically. It had good relations with the United States and a deep space tracking station would enhance them. But NASA could find no site technically satisfactory. A tracking station needs insulation from radio interference. The best location is a broad valley. The surrounding mountains shield the antenna. Japan's intensive land use left no valley free of radiowave pollution. The station went to Australia in the southern box.

In *The Politics of Space Cooperation* Don E. Kash describes a similar decision-making process leading to the selection of Nigeria as the site of a tracking and communication station for the Gemini series.[17] NASA sought a site in Africa for voice communication with the space craft just after launching from Cape Kennedy. While Kash does not use indifference curve analysis, his account may readily be seen in this way. The final consideration of both technical and political alternatives put two countries, Nigeria and Liberia, on the most north-eastern indifference curve. Other African countries fell on lower indifference curves.

The selection of sites for labor attaché conferences may also be explained in terms of indifference curve analysis. Every three to five years the ILAB likes to bring its labor attachés together for regional conferences.[18] The conferences allow an exchange of information between Washington and the field on a direct informal level, assure conformity with Labor Department policy, and boost morale. The conferences are paid for with excess currency generated from the sale of American agricultural products under the provisions of Public Law 480. Selecting a site for these labor attaché conferences involves two dimensions: the location's characteristics and the amount of Public Law 480 funds available. The chief characteristic sought in planning a conference is a central location. Next is the attitude of the country toward labor. Communist countries are beyond the pale because they do not have free labor unions. Third is the facilities available— does the embassy have enough conference rooms, can it arrange hotel accommodations, access to international transportation, etc. The final and easiest requirement is for security for any classified information. Whereas in the case of site selection for spacecraft tracking stations the two axes approximated the orientation of the two departments—NASA versus State—involved in the decision-making process, in this case the two axes approximate a labor affairs versus a budgetary dimension. In terms of departments this could be roughly expressed as Labor and State versus the Treasury, since the Treasury is the custodian of the PL 480 funds.

Figure 3-2 is an indifference map for the selection of the site for the 1969 European and African regional conference. In figure 3-2 several countries appear on indifference curve III. They were all equally desirable, or in this case, equally undesirable. Yugoslavia and Poland had Public Law 480 counterpart funds available but they were unacceptable locations because they were behind the Iron Curtain. France and Italy were good locations but had no Public Law 480 funds. The Congo and Guinea had some Public Law 480 funds but rated very low as desirable locations. Morocco was on curve II. It had sufficient funds but its location was poor. It was too far west for convenience. Tunisia, the site eventually chosen, was on curve I. Public Law 480 funds were available. The location was good; it was central. The country had a strong labor movement. The embassy was big enough to support a regional conference. Hotels and transportation were easily available in Tunis.

Figure 3-3 is a similar map for the 1970 Asian regional conference. Indonesia was on curve IV. It had no Public Law 480 funds and was a poor location. Israel was more desirable; at least funds were available. But in view of the explosive situation in the Middle East in 1970 Israel was too "hot" to use. Pakistan had Public Law 480 funds. Its location was better than Israel's but the embassy was small and there was no labor attaché. New Delhi, on curve I, was finally chosen. The Indian government had "a big pile of money" generated from wheat pur-

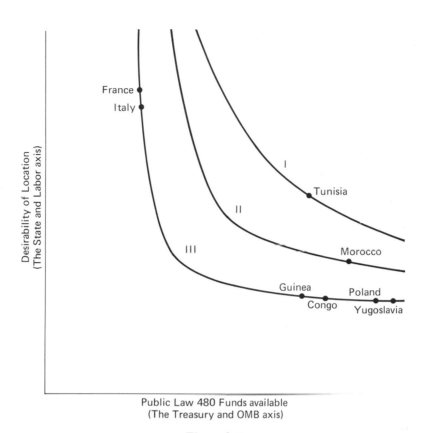

Figure 3-2.

chases. New Delhi was central. The embassy was willing to host the conference. The embassy was big and New Delhi had many hotels and good international transportation. Security was good. Best of all, the embassy had a "crackerjack labor attaché."

Writing in *Games and Decisions* Luce and Raiffa suggest that utility theory is not a good explanation of certain types of decision making.[19] Instead they propose a risk theory to explain these decisions. This is the equivalent of the minimax criterion proposed by L.J. Savage.[20] Under a risk theory the actor is more concerned with the risk of failure than the reward of success. Hence he acts to minimize his loss rather than to maximize his gain. Observers of the political scene have noted this type of behavior. A risk orientation leads to a much different pattern of behavior than a utility orientation. Among other things, it leads to under-optimizing production possibilities.

Two aspects of space technology applications suggest that the actors involved

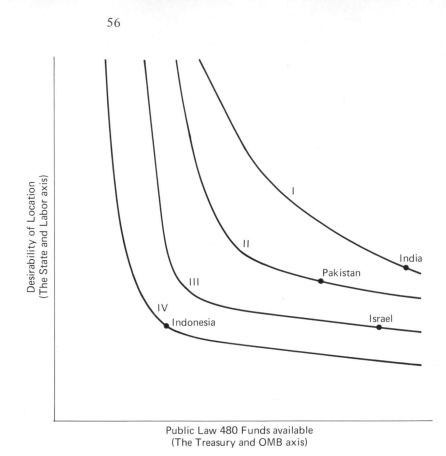

Figure 3–3.

are guided by risk rather than utility. First is in the Intelsat program. The users of the communication satellite system have insisted on redundancy.[21] They fear catastrophic failure. This failure could be natural, mechanical, or deliberate. The satellite might be hit by a meteor. It might fail mechanically. In the summer of 1969 the antenna, which spins to counter the spin of the satellite, froze on the Intelsat III on the Atlantic station. The satellite was out of operation for a month.[22] The satellite might be jammed by an enemy nation wishing to neutralize its military communication capacity. For these reasons the users have insisted on alternate channels of communication. Commercial users are concerned about the volume. Military users are concerned with keeping at least some communication at all times.

The second area suggesting risk orientation is cooperation with the U.S.S.R. The world's foremost space powers have almost no joint projects. The few exceptions to this U.S.-U.S.S.R. freeze on cooperation are nearly insignificant.

The exchange of meterologic data, the "cold line," yields little useful information. The data sent tends to be outdated and inferior to that obtained by the Nimbus satellites. The joint publication of biomedical research is a modest project only recently undertaken. The single instance of American-Soviet cooperation in space with even potential significance is the negotiations begun in Moscow in October 1970 between representatives of NASA and the Soviet Academy of Sciences to study means of docking their vehicles in space. This would make international rescue missions possible in emergency situations.[23] With these three exceptions, cooperation is virtually non-existant. One reason for the space cold war may be fear of disaster. Some secret might leak out allowing the other to gain a military or propaganda victory. Rather than utility, the two nations appear to be guided by a risk orientation.

4 Specialization

"The division of labor is limited by the extent of the market." This statement by Adam Smith offers the key to the amount of specialization in the foreign affairs arena. Smith notes that the division of labor enhances efficiency for three reasons. It allows the producers to develop greater skills. Time is not lost by switching from one job to another, and the specialized producer can afford to introduce efficient machinery. Increased specialization leads to increased exchange and increased exchange leads to increased specialization. And if done efficiently the process leads to enhanced total resources. Boulding notes that this principle extends far beyond the field usually covered by economics. For example, in science specialization (provided it is not carried to an extreme) leads to the fruitful exchange of knowledge.[1]

The expansion of the foreign affairs arena since World War II has allowed increased specialization. Before the war the Foreign Service had handled the bulk of America's small amount of foreign affairs business by itself. After the war, with the vast expansion of foreign involvement, the Foreign Service was unable to handle the volume. Other agencies stepped into the breach. The Labor Department supported the new labor attaché program. The Treasury enhanced its dominance over finance. Most important of all the military establishment, soon to emerge as the Department of Defense, took over a major portion of the State Department's pre-war arena. Today Adam Smith's axiom is still manifested in a multitude of examples. The State Department frequently must defer to the Treasury on matters of international monetary policy. It must defer because it lacks expertise; it lacks expertise because it enters the financial arena too seldom to justify developing its own specialists. International finance is a highly specialized field. To develop expertise a man must usually devote years to working in a narrow area. Within the State Department the demand is too small to allow this specialization. The department's rotation policy denies a man the long tenure necessary to develop his skills. Framed in terms of Smith's three rules, the FSO fails to develop skills, loses effectiveness by switching from one job to another, and cannot introduce capital equipment such as computers because of the small scale of his operations.

The Humphrey amendment to the Foreign Assistance Act of 1961 was an attempt by the Congress to secure some of the advantages of specialization. The amendment provided that foreign assistance in fields where domestic agencies had competence would be performed by these agencies.[2] Rather than obtain its own specialists directly, AID would obtain them from the domestic agencies.

The Labor Department would supply labor advisors. The IRS would supply tax experts. The Office of Education would send educational consultants. In Smith's terms the Humphrey amendment expanded the foreign assistance market so that greater specialization could occur.

While the extent of the market determines the amount of specialization, its form is often determined by organizations outside the agency. Specialization can be structured by other agencies in Washington or overseas, by private institutions, by professional disciplines, by geography, by language or by the level of production.

Each of the three domestic departments studied has an international office. To a large extent the purpose of this office is to deal with the State Department. Thus an agency develops a specialty of dealing with another agency. This is even more obvious in the establishment of congressional liaison offices which explicitly specialize in relations with another branch of government.

At times the State Department seems to be little more than an agglomeration of contact points. The country desks handle contacts with the embassies. The Labor Office deals with the Labor Department. The Science Bureau deals with NASA and the NSF. The International Monetary Affairs division of the Economic Bureau deals with the Treasury. An official interviewed from this division estimated that he spent 75 percent of his day dealing with outside agencies and only 25 percent dealing with other State Department offices. Of the time spent with outside agencies, 60 percent was with the Treasury, 20 percent with interagency working groups and 20 percent in direct bilateral discussions with five other agencies. Within the State Department he assisted country and regional economic officers in complex financial matters like debt rescheduling and currency exchange rate. In a sense the International Monetary division has no independent existence. It depends entirely on other agencies in and out of the State Department for its *raison d'être*.

The Treasury as well depends on other government agencies for defining its specialties. The chief domestic one is the Federal Reserve System. The Treasury's International Office is routinely in contact with the Federal Reserve to exchange money, information, and other bureaucratic commodities to assist in the American balance of payments position. Treasury specialization is further defined by the foreign treasuries and central banks. Treasury officials interviewed were highly impressed by, even envious of, the financial specialty in European countries. They pointed to these institutions as models for the U.S. Treasury to emulate. The British Treasury is the acme. The post of First Lord of the Treasury is held by the prime minister himself. He and the Chancellor of the Exchequer prepare the annual government budget secretly with little interference from the rest of the Cabinet. The highly autonomous Bank of England was under private ownership until 1946.[3] The Treasury officials interviewed held the other European countries's treasuries and central banks in equally high esteem. The French post of Inspecteur des Finances was established by Napoleon. The

"Rue de Rivoli" has always dominated the civil service, exercising a leadership function similar to that of the British Treasury. The children of the aristocratic families aspire to enter the Finance Ministry above all others.[4] In the Netherlands the finance minister is more important than the prime minister. Views such as these, whether or not they are an accurate picture of foreign treasuries, do indicate the extent to which the American Treasury tries to model itself after the European agencies.

NASA is fostering a structuring of foreign government agencies which is the reciprocal of the Treasury copying of foreign patterns. When NASA signs a cooperative agreement with a foreign country one of the conditions on which it insists is that the foreign government designate a single agency to implement the agreement. Since few countries already have a space agency of their own this means that they must establish one. This is usually done within an existing science or technology ministry. Thus all over the world, governments are giving birth to baby NASAs. Argentina has established a National Commission for Space Research. India has a Space Research Organization. Pakistan has SUPARCO, the Space and Upper Atmosphere Research Committee.[5] The form of their division of labor is following that of an outside agency.

Private institutions both at home and abroad can determine the form of specialization. The AFL and the CIO, now merged, were strong supporters of the labor attaché program when it emerged after the Second World War. In the early days many of the labor attachés and labor advisors were recruited directly from organized labor rather than from the FSO corps as now. The Truman administration encouraged direct trade union involvement. As a result the Marshall Plan was more oriented toward trade unions than labor ministries. During the late 1950s and the early 1960s the labor specialty returned to greater State Department control. The brashness of many of the labor specialists recruited from the AFL-CIO alienated both their host governments and the regular Foreign Service. They neglected the basic economic conditions behind labor problems. They aroused expectations among foreign workers that could not be met. At the same time the political power of the AFL-CIO waned at home.

The labor attaché program owes its firm establishment to a foreign organization. At the end of the war the program was still experimental. Only two labor attachés had ever been assigned—one to Buenos Aires and one to London. In the spring of 1945 the American embassy in London was caught unprepared by the upset victory of the Labour Party. None of the diplomats had cultivated relations with the newly elected party. The embassy's savior in the face of this switch from stripped pants to cloth cap was the young labor attaché, Samuel Berger. He alone knew the Labour leaders who inherited Whitehall from the Churchill government. His contacts tided over the embassy in what would otherwise have been a difficult transition.[6]

The structure of industry can determine the internal structure of the bureaucracy. The subdivision of the Economic Bureau into its various offices follows the subdivision of American industry. The bureau has an Office of Food Policy, an Office of Fuels, a Fibers and Textiles Division, an Office of Aviation, an Office of Telecommunications, and an Office of Maritime Affairs. Organizing along industry lines has an inherent logic. It is easy to define. Tariffs have traditionally been by product, and clientele groups are organized along these lines.

The bureaucratic division of labor both follows and cuts across professional lines. Economists are concentrated in certain agencies and bureaus. The Treasury and the State Department's Economic Bureau are the particular domains of this profession. Yet economists are also scattered throughout other bureaus. They are found in the regional geographic bureaus of the State Department and in the Labor Department. Officials interviewed remarked on the professional commonality of the economists. Several noted that there was more conflict between economists within the State Department than between the different departments. Economists in the geographic bureaus form a fifth column willing to betray their own bureaus in the interests of their profession. They are prone to pass on intelligence to aid their allies in the Economic Bureau plan strategy advancing policies based on sound economics. The Economic Bureau itself constitutes a fifth column willing to convey intelligence to the Treasury when it would advance its own position within the State Department.

Within the State Department's Science Bureau specialization follows the forms of the professional demarcations of science. The Bureau has offices of Atomic Energy, Environment, and Space-Atmosphere and Marine Affairs. This professional categorizing is reminiscent of the Economic Bureau's industrial specialization.

Geography structures the division of labor of all federal agencies in the foreign affairs arena. With the presumption of the Renaissance pope who once divided the world between Spain and Portugal, the State Department has divided the world into five geographic regions. These regions are Europe, Africa, Latin America, East Asia, and the Near East and South Asia. International organizations constitute a sixth "region." The State Department has imposed this six part division of the globe on all its constituent agencies and bureaus. AID, USIA, and the Peace Corps all follow it. So do its Bureaus of Educational and Cultural Affairs and of Intelligence and Research. The Labor Department uses the identical breakdown in the ILAB. The Treasury uses a modified version.

The State Department does offer a second specialized structure which partially counteracts the rigidity of its six part geographic division. This is language. While the geographic structure does have the sublime beauty of inherent logic, it does not lend itself too well to the limited abilities of a single man to master all the languages of a region. Thus an FSO will develop a language proficiency that will constitute a personal specialty.[7] His assignments will be limited to countries speaking the one or two foreign languages in which he can attain fluency. An officer proficient in French will have a career in the Metropole and Francophonie. This will cut across the geographic regions of Europe, Africa, and East

Asia. One proficient in Arabic will have a career in Africa and the Near East regions. Such an FSO will have the privilege of calling himself an Arabist. Today, just as twenty years ago, an FSO once more has the option of being an "old China hand." This specialty, which went out of style in the McCarthy era, has been reborn under the aegis of President Nixon's visit to China.

Within the total foreign policy bureaucracy certain bureaus (and certain individuals) specialize according to their level of production. Labor is divided according to the degree to which the bureaucratic commodities are transformed. Certain bureaus (and bureaucrats) specialize in trading the basic commodities of Group 1. Others specialize in manufacturing the refined commodities of Group 3. Those who trade Group 1 commodities are bureaucratic brokers. They take market forces where they find them and try to arrange an exchange on this basis. Others add some input of their own, assembling or refining Group 1 commodities into one of Group 2 or Group 3. Some specialize in inventing new commodities of Group 4.

AID specializes in trading. It is a brokerage agency. It performs its assignment by contracting with other agencies and private organizations to perform its tasks for it. AID gets labor advisors from the DOLITAC. It gets tax advisors from the Internal Revenue Service. It builds dams in Afganistan by arranging for a private corporation to construct them. AID officials interviewed were enthusiastic about their brokerage specialization. They cited its advantage of being able to draw upon the most qualified experts and resources in each area, without the overhead of maintaining these expert personnel and resources when they are not needed. A statistician can return to the Bureau of Labor Statistics when he comes back from abroad. A school administrator can return to the Office of Education. Several respondents in other agencies expressed envy for the AID contractual procedure.

The geographic subdivisions of the ILAB, the Treasury, and the State Department tend to specialize in assembling commodities. They do more than merely exchanging commodities as they find them. They do some rearranging of their own, sorting, shuffling, or combining to produce a Group 2 commodity. The State Department's desk officers and domestic agencies regional officers work to achieve continuity. They try to eliminate conflicting programs. They believe the total American policy toward a country should be integrated.

The individual information officers in the four agencies tend to have specialized in this second level of production. They face two directions. Outwardly they specialize in assembling information for news reporters. Inwardly they specialize in intelligence gathering. While this internal sleuthing is not in their Civil Service Commission job description it is a function highly prized by their bosses.

The Bureau of Labor Statistics specializes in manufacturing refined commodities. It does not engage in brokerage or assemblage of data. The labor attachés do this for it. Rather it concentrates on refining this data into statistics suitable for use by other agencies. The State Department's Economic Bureau also specializes in this level of production. The embassy economic officers gather the information and send it via the geographic bureaus to the Economic Bureau for refining.

The State Department specializes in representation. This includes diplomatic negotiations with foreign governments. It also includes handling complaints. When a country is offended or hurt by a U.S. policy it goes to the American embassy to complain. The embassy forwards the complaint to Washington where the State Department takes up the cause. The domestic departments accuse the State Department of encouraging these complaints.

NASA specializes in the production of the invented commodities of Group 4. As mentioned in chapter 2, NASA is primarily a research and development agency. Once a project is past this stage NASA transfers it to a performance agency. The performance agency will reimburse NASA for routine services thereafter but not for the developmental cost. Thus Comsat Corporation pays NASA each time it launches a communication satellite but has not paid for the costs of developing the satellite in the first place. The National Aeronautical and Space Act of 1958 provided for this sort of specialization by the new agency. The Communication Satellite Act of 1962 made the division of labor between the space agency and the corporation more explicit.[8]

The advantages of specialization are mirrored by the disadvantages of segmentation. Each specialty walls itself in from its neighbors. The total system becomes disjointed. Each special compartment will be narrowly oriented only toward its own interests. The State Department administrative division of the world into the geographic regions has its counterpart in differing foreign policy toward each region. The Latin American region is the most independent of the six. The State Department's Latin American Bureau has been fully integrated with those of AID and USIA. This autonomy works both to strengthen the joint bureau internally and to isolate it further from the other geographic bureaus. The combined bureau administers the Alliance for Progress. Its chief holds the dual post of Assistant Secretary and U.S. Coordinator for the Alliance. The theme of the Latin American Bureau is economic development. The top officials are interested and well trained in economics. Even senior FSOs brought up in the old school of pure diplomacy have become interested in development. AID's inclusion puts the means close at hand. The economics is straightforward. It generates statistics suitable for score keeping. Country X has a growth rate of 4 percent. Country Y increased its GNP by three billion dollars. The Treasury seldom enters into Latin American affairs. It is not interested in development but in finance. It generally agrees with the State Department policy of encouraging growth. It has a limited number of experts and prefers not to dissipate its manpower in the underdeveloped areas of the world.

The Treasury's involvement in the European Bureau is much different. The Treasury is interested in Europe since this is where the financial action is. Unlike the combined Latin American Bureau the European Bureau includes only the State Department portion. The USIA is separate and AID no longer has a European program. The senior officials and the FSOs who staff the bureau emphasize traditional diplomacy. They are neither oriented toward nor trained in economics. This, combined with the complexities of European economics and finance, means that the bureau is dependent on the Treasury for its expertise. The Treasury, for its part, is eager to enter the European scene. It concentrates its limited manpower here. The consequence is geographically segmented policies. Foreign policy toward Latin America encourages economic development. The State Department dominates. Policy toward Europe is financial. The Treasury dominates.

American policy toward East Asia has had a third set of characteristics. The military has dominated since World War II. The occupation policies toward Japan and Germany reflected this dichotomy in the immediate post-war era. Under the vice-regency of General MacArthur, Japan continued to be governed by the military until 1952. Germany, on the other hand, was a civilian province. The military government surrendered control to a State Department High Commissioner in 1949.[9] Today the Vietnamese war is a continuing reminder of the military dominance of policy toward East Asia.

John Harr observes that State Department ideology restricts an FSO's freedom to specialize. Certain fields are approved while others are taboo. Acceptable specialties are the political, most economic, political-military, and international organizational affairs. Non-acceptable fields include aid, information, labor, and finance. The willingness of an FSO to specialize in a given field is often a product of the attitude which favors the "generalist" over the "specialist." Those who specialize in the first set of fields are still considered to be "generalists" while those who choose from the second are "specialists," hence of a lower status. Besides Foreign Service ideology, there is the career factor. Promotions tend to go more to those in the mainstream, not to the marginal "specialists."[10]

The State Department's tendency to represent foreign interests is a function of its specialization. Each of the domestic agencies has a particular domestic clientele whose interests it advances. The State Department lacks a domestic clientele but does have a foreign one. A young FSO learns that one way to advance in his career is to earn a reputation for satisfying foreign governments. This is much less true for any one of the sixteen Treasury representatives abroad because they have a much lower investment in a foreign career. If the foreign government does not achieve satisfaction at the American embassy, it can circumvent the embassy by channeling its complaints through its own embassy in Washington. Although the American embassy has "failed" because it has lost a client, the complaint still goes through. Rather than fail, the embassy in the field prefers to keep the account by pressing the complaint more vigorously with Washington.

The disadvantages of segmentation can occur as a result of the division of labor based on the level of production. NASA is an inventive agency. It stresses goal achievement. The State Department is not inventive. Among other things, it stresses conformity to a single foreign policy. The segmentation puts the two agencies in a state of continual tension. The State Department wants conformity while NASA wants performance. Conformity includes respecting the Intelsat monopoly and not launching rockets in the Near East. Performance means disregarding the Intelsat monopoly and launching probes from Israel. The State Department observes strict security (though not as strict as the Defense Department). NASA tries only not to betray military secrets. State is cautious; NASA is daring. The tension is built in.

Andrew Scott suggests that segmentation may work its mischief on a grand scale. He argues that the entire State Department has walled itself off from its environment. It has isolated itself from interaction with new elements that threaten to disturb its internal tranquility. Since the environment cannot impinge on the organization, pressure for adaptation is reduced. The demands on the organization to operate efficiently decline. New techniques of research, management, and planning are some of the environmental challenges that the State Department seeks to close out of its system. This isolation of Foggy Bottom has brought on an overall decline of the department relative to the other departments with which it competes in the foreign affairs arena. Furthermore, by this segmentation "its ability to reach out and mobilize support when it needs it is also reduced."[11]

Jurisdiction and Monopoly

"The State Department has a monopoly in foreign affairs." This opinion is expressed so often and so fervently by officials of the Department that it seems that they must swear a blood oath to it as an article of faith before being admitted to the brotherhood. This alleged monopoly is the first article in the FSOs' creed and the final argument in an interdepartmental meeting when a rival agency threatens to infringe on State Department prerogatives. The State Department has developed a metaphysics to justify the claim to monopoly. It revolves around dualities like "function versus policy" or "technical versus political." It refers frequently to "sovereignty" and "constitutional role." The Department's defense of its monopoly brings it into constant jurisdictional battles with the domestic agencies. Interviewees frequently complained of other agencies refusing to respect their jurisdiction: "Many domestic agencies feel that they should play a stronger role in foreign policy, but Congress has been very clear on this point. Their role is functional, not policy." "All action is policy but some technical people do not realize the policy implications of their actions." "Some technicians have not been well informed on the U.S. position." Witnesses appearing before the Jackson subcommittee voiced these same laments of lack of respect for the State Department's titular monopoly.[1]

Orthodox Foggy Bottom dogma proclaims that the State Department holds sway over all foreign lands. Its jurisdiction begins at the water's edge; at this same point the jurisdictions of all other agencies end. These other agencies, however, often invade the State Department's domain when their own interests carry them abroad.

Among the three departments studied the Treasury poses the greatest challenge to the State Department. It has successfully invaded the State Department's jurisdiction to the point where it has virtually a free hand in international finance. The present spheres of influence have been in existence in essentially the same form since at least the 1930s. Several respondents attributed this division to State Department disinterest in finance under Secretary of State Cordell Hull. The right of the Treasury to manage international finance was formalized in the Bretton Woods conference. This 1944 meeting, which set up the present international monetary system, was presided over by Secretary of the Treasury Henry Morganthau. The Treasury ran the meeting while the State Department watched. Secretary John Connally's strong role in the 1971 dollar crisis reiterated the Treasury's dominant position.

While the Treasury has dominated international finance for four decades, the exact boundaries between its sphere and the State Department's have been continually redefined. One dimension along which this occurs is the degree of specificity of a financial policy. The Treasury has more autonomy when the policy is specific. The State Department is more prone to enter the process when the policy is general. A bilateral treaty on double taxation is specific. Its effects can be accurately foreseen. Its terms can be tailored to the individual country. The State Department receives few complaints. A change in American monetary policy, however, is general. Its effects cannot always be foreseen nor can they be limited. They effect many countries. Countries hurt by the policy change complain to the State Department which in turn complains to the Treasury.

The State Department complaints come as no surprise. The two departments have been fighting skirmishes along the border between finance and international relations for so long that they have developed a set of mutual role expectations. In this and in other areas each department knows the position of its counterpart, or in the words of one Treasury official: "They don't surprise us. I have been in the international game for thirty years and I know how the State Department thinks." Another official noted the mutual role expectations based on established spheres of influence. Speaking of finance, he said: "In this field, they recognize that we are the ones who run the show and they defer to us." This recognition of Treasury dominance of finance is not rampant aggrandizement. The Treasury is willing to recognize that certain areas belong to the State Department. A third Treasury official said, "Finance has been our sphere much as trade and aid has been in the State Department's sphere of influence." State Department respondents voiced corresponding attitudes toward the Treasury. One FSO observed that "in finance, the Treasury has the responsibility." A colleague of his remarked that "the Treasury will usually go along in trade; this is not the case in the financial area."

The balance of payments is another area which the State Department leaves to the Treasury. The Secretary of the Treasury heads a cabinet committee responsible for this. The Under Secretary of Monetary Affairs heads the U.S. delegation to Working Party 3 of the Organization for Economic Cooperation and Development (OECD). WP3, as it is known informally, is concerned with balance of payments.[2] Like the under secretary, the delegates from the European nations are representatives of their countries' financial ministries or central banks, never of their foreign ministries. Financiers do not trust diplomats in matters as serious as money. Interviewees at the Treasury stressed the low values they accord to State Department input into financial policy making. With great condescension one acknowledged that "the State Department is allowed to sit in when we write position papers for the OECD."

The State Department also leaves all matters pertaining to taxation and customs to the Treasury. Within the Treasury the responsibility for tax policy is split between the IRS and the staff of the Assistant Secretary for Tax Policy in Office of the Secretary. Customs, being less controversial, is not represented in the Office of the Secretary. The Bureau of Customs handles policy making as well as operations.

While the Treasury has jurisdiction in finance, tax, and customs, the State Department claims trade and aid. State's dominance in trade dates back to the tenure of Secretary Hull. As one long-time bureaucrat put it: "Cordell Hull had a one-track mind." He was obsessed by reciprocal trade, so obsessed that he neglected other aspects of economic policy. The Treasury displays a reverse attitude toward trade. It considers it nonessential to its sphere of influence; therefore it can be left to the diplomats. Responsibility for the 1965 U.S.-Canadian agreement on automobile manufacturing fell to the State Department. This agreement eliminated duties on automobile parts. The components can be shipped freely across the border to assembly factories. Under the agreement an automobile can just as easily be manufactured in Ontario as Michigan.[3]

Foreign aid is the other major economic area in which the State Department has managed to impose its formal monopoly. AID is now under the control of the Secretary of State. The State Department has managed to tame it since the early days of European recovery when the ECA ran a rival foreign affairs ministry with "embassies" in the major European capitals. Even in those days the Treasury never had much interest in the aid program. Today, with AID's declining influence and sluggish budget, the State Department is in firmer control than at any previous time.

The Treasury does enter the foreign aid field when the aid is multilateral. These international lending institutions include the World Bank, the Inter-American Development Bank, the International Development Association, and the Asian Bank.[4] The Treasury shepherds the appropriations bills for these international banks through Congress. This gives it control of the funds once approved.

The State Department has been much more successful in defending its titular foreign affairs monopoly against the Labor Department than it has been against the Treasury. In part the State Department could resist the Labor Department encroachment because State had already sold out to the trade unions. As mentioned previously, the AFL and the CIO dominated the labor attaché and labor assistance programs in the post-war period. During the 1950s important labor attachés assignments had to pass muster by a three man committee including Phil Delaney, who was the union's man in Foggy Bottom. Today the AFL-CIO participation is declining. This may indicate lessened influence or it may merely indicate general approval with the program. Until his recent retirement Delaney continued to look after the union's interests. Today small posts are filled routinely, but the assignment of a labor attaché to a major embassy in Europe still calls for State's Labor Office and the ILAB to consult informally with 16th Street. State and Labor try to anticipate the AFL-CIO reaction.

Whereas the Treasury has deprived the State Department completely of certain segments of its formal jursidiction, the Labor Department has been unable to wrest away territory to be totally its own. The Treasury enjoys nearly complete autonomy in finance, tax, customs, and multilateral aid. The Labor Department can only make contributions in the labor area. The State Department retains jurisdiction. Joseph R. Fiszman has analyzed the position of the labor attaché caught between the pressures of the two departments to which he is responsible.[5] He concludes that the labor attaché tends to favor the State Department and slight the Labor Department. Fiszman attributes this to the labor attachés membership in the Foreign Service corps. The personnel affiliation influences his job orientation. He favors the agency that will eventually decide whether or not to promote him. While this may be a satisfactory explanation of his individual view of the career system, in fact the Labor Department seems to derive a greater benefit from having the labor attaché on station. To the State Department, the labor attaché is just another information gatherer, one of many in the political or economic section of the embassy. But to the Labor Department, the attaché is its very own agent. He gathers information which it values highly, and represents "labor" both internally in the embassy and externally to the people of that country. This can be seen in terms of utility. The labor attaché dedicates a greater proportion of his efforts toward satisfying the State Department, but that department places a low utility on this contribution. He makes less of an effort toward satisfying the Labor Department, but the Labor Department places a high utility on this smaller contribution. Furthermore, the ILAB is more skillful in capitalizing on the attaché's work. It asks him more questions. The questions are better prepared. It knows which foreign labor leader he should contact. It knows which foreign factories manufacture exports competing with American workers' production.

The State Department has been most successful defending its foreign affairs jurisdiction against the incursions of NASA. One weapon in its arsenal has been its mythology. It has succeeded in convincing NASA that it (State) alone can operate in this arena. One NASA scientist stated, in respectfully hushed tones, that the State Department was the only agency capable of negotiating for a tracking station because it involved "sovereignty": "Since these are agreements which include sovereignty they have to be done on inter-governmental level. This is followed by an interagency agreement." This lack of sophistication as to the contribution of the State Department would never have been voiced at the Treasury, where disregard for the State Department's monopoly is routine. The Treasury is used to invading the State Department territory whenever and wherever it has the interest, the expertise and the manpower to do so. NASA is much more respectful.

NASA is greatly involved with the work of the U.N. Space Committees. Here, as in negotiations for tracking stations, NASA defers to the State Department. "The State Department has the responsibility for action." Despite this humility NASA does contribute extensively to managing the American participation in the committee. Its international office is in daily contact with the International

Organization Bureau preparing instructions. These then go to the U.S. delegation at New York to guide its participation at the committee meetings. The Space Committee has two subcommittees. One is legal and one is technical. NASA's Assistant Administrator for International Affairs is the delegate to the technical subcommittee. Although the subcommittee is technical and he is selected for his technical competence, a NASA official gave assurances that "he is bound by State Department policy." With NASA behaving with such deference Foggy Bottom has little to fear in jurisdictional skirmishes with the space agency.

One exception to this general tranquility along the State-NASA frontier centers on the launch capability for Intelsat. NASA is concerned for three reasons. First, it developed the communication satellite originally. Second, it continues to launch the satellites. And third, the launching service ties in with some of NASA's planned projects. NASA plans to build a space shuttle. This will be a large, reusable vehicle designed to ferry astronaut-scientists and equipment to and from a permanent earth orbiting space station. Because the shuttle is expensive and because the NASA budget is declining, the agency has been seeking money from European countries. Administrator Thomas O. Paine went to Bonn in 1969 to offer the Germans a 10 percent interest for seven years. Paine has tried to sell the shuttle to seven other countries.[6] The Europeans seemed quite interested but conditioned their participation on breaking into the Intelsat monopoly. NASA is much more willing to sell out Intelsat than the State Department is. Intelsat presents a combination of a political and an economic monopoly. Politically the United States wants an Intelsat monopoly because control over the flow of information enhances its national security position. Economically the United States wants the monopoly because it believes that the market is not large enough to support two systems. In either case an Intelsat monopoly is not really a U.S. monopoly. The Intelsat Corporation is owned by the member countries. The U.S. representative is the Comsat Corporation. Ownership is based on the volume of traffic. When it was first organized the American share was 60 percent. By 1970 it was down to 52 percent. By the end of 1972 it will be down to 40 percent.

The State Department's Economic Bureau fully backs the economic monopoly aspects of Intelsat. One FSO compared it to a public utility corporation like the telephone company or water company. Duplication would be wasteful. A global system is necessary to achieve economies of scale. There would be more contributors to start the system and more customers once it was started. Coordination would be better. Finally it would have a global outlook. Among other things this would give the underdeveloped nations a role. The alternative is a disjointed network of parochial national satellites.

Intelsat does allow for certain types of communication satellites outside the program, providing that they are not directly competing. Intelsat permits other satellites which are domestic, regional or specialized. Canada has a domestic satellite for communication within its boundaries. Europe is planning a regional television satellite for the European Television Union.

The Economic Bureau feels that the French initiated Symphonie project threatens the Intelsat monopoly. The French claim that it is purely a regional satellite permitted by the Intelsat Consortium. It has designed the satellite, whose name means to unite a language, to join France with the French-speaking nations overseas. It would connect the Metropole with Francophone Africa and Martinique and Haiti in the West Indies. More significantly it would also service Quebec. Indo-China would not be included because it is beyond the broadcast range of a single satellite. The Economic Bureau feels that this is competitive with Intelsat. The French counter that it is not because there would not be this traffic without a Symphonie. Production of the satellite is a joint undertaking of France, Germany, and Belgium. Germany claims that the program is experimental. It is participating solely to enhance its research and development capabilities. The French goal, however, is operational.

The big issue with the Symphonie is who will put it into orbit. Symphonie's builders have three possibilities. First, they could develop an independent European launch capability. The Europeans have established the European Launch Development Organization (ELDO). ELDO operates from an Australian range. By 1970 it had had eleven straight failures and no successes. Secondly, they could buy launches from the United States on a mission by mission basis. This would be cheaper but it would mean accepting the American monopoly. The United States could veto any satellite that failed to satisfy it. Thirdly, they could buy a share of the U.S. launch capability. This would be more expensive than the second method but it would insure that the United States would be required to launch any satellite. This third method ties in with NASA's search for money to build the space shuttle. The Europeans want their contributions to the shuttle, which is research oriented, to give them a more immediate return in the practical matter of communication satellites. NASA is more willing to do this than is the State Department.

A fourth possibility is remote but still exists. The Russians may be willing to launch the Symphonie. Russia has not expressed any specific willingness to do so, but it has an agreement to launch a French scientific satellite.

The American dilemma is a typical one for a monopolist. It wants to get the highest price in terms of conformity to the Intelsat system and contribution to the American launch capability. But it cannot demand too high a price for to do so would drive the Europeans to develop their own rival launch capability or to reach an agreement with the Russians. Strictly speaking, this is a case of monopolistic competition rather than pure monopoly. If the price the United States demands goes too high the Europeans do have possible alternatives.[7]

Jonathan F. Galloway has noted that in becoming the coordinator in Intelsat, the State Department was actually expanding its jurisdiction.[8] Previously it had left international communication to the private telegraph companies and had performed simply the most perfunctory services of legitimizing their contractual arrangements.

The State Department moved into the space communication field because it recognized this new bureaucratic territory would be a valuable resource. NASA's pioneering had opened up a new frontier and the State Department took the opportunity to do some homesteading. There was no particular reason that the same commercial arrangements that controlled transoceanic communication could not be extended to space. But the space program had opened up some virgin territory and one of the rules of bureaucratic homesteading is first come, first served. The private telegraph companies were timid. They held back while the State Department grabbed the territory. The State Department could not have managed this land grab without a few resources of its own. Chief among these was its jurisdiction over foreign affairs. Foggy Bottom based its claim to regulate communication satellites on this right. One serious rival domestically was the Federal Communications Commission. The FCC based its claim on its jurisdiction over radio broadcasts. In the final arrangements the FCC retained a right to veto at three levels. The Commission must approve a satellite's construction, its launching, and its operation. It must also approve construction of ground facilities.[9]

Comsat Corporation was the State Department's most troublesome competitor for bureaucratic space. The corporation wanted the freedom to make its own arrangements without State Department interference. In December 1962 the Chairman of the Board, Philip L. Graham, quarrelled with the Department. He accused it of "meddling."[10] The Department was able to prevail over Comsat through a two pronged attack. First it appealed to its mythology of a monopoly in foreign affairs. It claimed that since Comsat was "the chosen instrument of U.S. foreign policy" it should receive policy guidance from the Department. Second, it claimed that it represented the views of the European members (at that time potential members). In this it was capitalizing on its specialty of representing foreigners. In the end Comsat came to accept the State Department dominance. NASA was never interested in competing with the State Department for jurisdiction in this area. The private telegraph companies were left too far behind to compete.

The State Department's expansion into the area of satellite communication is one example of how an agency can extend its jurisdiction. There are other similar cases where changing conditions bring about new bureaucratic boundaries. These changes may be technological, as in the communication satellite instance, or they may be due to a crisis or to economic growth.

The American balance of payments crisis of the 1960s brought about an expansion of bureaucratic territories. Choice of air transportation for federal employees had formerly been unregulated. With a deteriorating balance of payments position the government ordered all employees traveling on official business to fly American flag carriers. More significantly the government began to intervene in the capital market. President Johnson ordered voluntary restrictions on investment abroad. Later he changed these guidelines to mandatory controls.

He directed the Federal Reserve banks to enforce the restrictions.[11] The Federal Reserve thereby acquired a new area of jurisdiction. This new territory proved too much for the manpower of the Federal Reserve banks. They were unable to administer the program.

Economic growth can open up new areas for agency expansion. At present foreign banks are trying to move into the American market. Because of the United States' federal structure they must get permission from the individual states to open new branches. Certain states have arbitrarily denied them permission to do business. When this has happened they have complained to the Treasury and the Federal Reserve. One possible solution is for Congress to expand the jurisdiction of either the Treasury or the Federal Reserve System to cover regulation of foreign banks.

Another emerging territory for agency expansion is the regulation of internationally based mutual funds. The irresponsible management of the IOS and the Gramco funds focused attention on this sub-area of foreign investment.[12] The Treasury has revealed no interest in regulating mutual funds. The State Department has taken some tentative steps in that direction.

While new technology crises and economic growth can add new territory for agency expansion, at the same time the creation of a new agency can ignite a set of jurisdiction skirmishes to reassign existing territory previously stabilized. The establishment of the Special Trade Representative in the Executive Office of the President did this. President Kennedy created the office under the provisions of the Trade Expansion Act of 1962. The function of the STR was to supervise and coordinate U.S. foreign trade policy. This put it squarely into the territory that had been the State Department's since the days of Secretary Hull. Prior to 1963 an FSO had chaired the interdepartmental committee which the STR inherited. Fortunately for the State Department, the office has only a small staff which is unable to handle its full responsibilities.

This competition between the State Department and the other agencies for jurisdiction over bureaucratic territory in the foreign affairs arena is analogous to the competition between firms for market territory. When the territory is unlimited each firm will seek to maximize its return by locating just outside the range of a competitor. The newcomer locates outside the territory of the first firm to avoid competing with it but at the same time it locates as close as possible to avoid leaving a gap that might attract a third firm to try to fill the vacuum, thereby competing with both.[13]

To some extent the behavior of agencies in the foreign affairs arena has followed this pattern. The rapid expansion of American participation in foreign affairs since World War II made bureaucratic territory virtually unlimited for a time. When the foreign affairs arena was expanded with the creation of a foreign aid program, AID's predecessor, the ECA, could take over this territory without infringing on the State Department's jurisdiction. When foreign affairs came to include propaganda, the USIA could similarly take over this territory without infringing on State's prerogatives. Thus the vast growth in American involvement overseas produced a series of coexisting monopolies not competing with each other.

Economists note, however, that the situation is much different when market territory is limited. Here the newcomer must challenge the original firm, carving its market space out of the territory of the latter. When the total market territory available is sufficient the two firms can arrive at a stable modus vivendi. If not, the two firms enter a battle for survival until the weaker succumbs. The best strategy for a newcomer seeking to challenge an established firm is to "make your product as like the existing products as you can without destroying the differences." This is the principle of minimum differentiation.[14]

The establishment of a competing foreign service by the Treasury is consistent with the principle of minimum differentiation. The sixteen Treasury representatives stationed in the embassies abroad closely resemble the Foreign Service economic officers. Both are concerned with business conditions, balance of payments problems, currency convertability, etc. But the Treasury tries to maintain the distinctiveness of its representatives, thereby assuring that they will not be merged into the Foreign Service.

When a third firm enters the competition for limited market territory, the problem becomes much more complicated. One of the chief complications is the possibility of a coalition forming. When three firms are competing for survival, two may gang up on the third. The two "outside" firms may be able to eliminate the "in-between" firm quite easily.[15]

A number of situations suggest that this is the strategy that the State Department follows when challenged by a bureaucratic competitor in the foreign affairs arena. The development of the labor attaché program connotes that the State Department chose to ally with organized labor rather than let the Labor Department emerge as the governmental sponsor of the labor attachés. A coalition with the trade unions seemed preferable to competition with them, either alone or in coalition with the Labor Department.

In negotiating the terms for coalitions the State Department often appears willing to relinquish a large quantity of substantive commodities providing that it maintains its titular jurisdiction. The State Department values the myth of foreign policy primacy more than the reality. The State Department's official monopoly frequently seems hollow in terms of the resources it is able to mobilize. Even when the State Department monopoly has been eaten away, as in finance, the department sticks to the rationale that those areas are nonessential "specialities." Foggy Bottom doctrine centers on maintaining the department as an umbrella over all activites in the arena. What transpires under the umbrella is open to compromise. Thus in bargaining with other departments the State Department sometimes appears to be more concerned with deference to its right to lead than with any particular direction in which to lead.

Bargaining

In their interaction with one another in exchange relationships the State Department and the three domestic departments studied engage in bargaining in market places ranging in their degree of organization from a highly structured interagency committee established by Congress to an unstructured network of personnel operating in the same commodity set.

The Board of the Foreign Service is among the most highly structured of these bureaucratic market places. Operating under the provisions of the Foreign Service Act of 1946 as amended, the Board is composed of assistant secretary level representatives for the State Department, AID, USIA, and the departments of Labor, Agriculture, and Commerce. Beneath the main board are a series of lesser boards charged with the more practical aspects of administering the Foreign Service. The Board of Examiners is one of these. It is responsible for the recruitment and selection of new Foreign Service Officers. Promotion boards are of this sort also.[1] It is at this level that the day to day bargaining takes place among the agencies. The department representative skilled in log-rolling can help along the career of one of his own. The Labor Department board member can enhance the promotion changes for a labor attaché through his bargaining tactics.

The National Advisory Council on International Monetary and Financial Policies is a slightly less formal bureaucratic market place. Established at the time of the Bretton Woods agreements, it now includes permanent representatives from the Treasury, State, Commerce, the Federal Reserve System, and the Export-Import Bank.[2] The Treasury representative chairs the meetings. The duties of the NAC are to approve or disapprove the transactions of the international banking institutions and to recommend to the Secretary of the Treasury instructions for U.S. delegations to international financial bodies. The Council meets weekly at the staff level. Sessions run two to three hours. Ten to thirty attend. Besides the permanent members these include extra representatives from the international banking institutions, from the State Department country desks, from AID, and from the U.S. directorates of the international banks.

Prior to the creation of the National Security Council, the NAC's jurisdiction included foreign aid. Now its jurisdiction is smaller, but due to the growth in the business of the international banks its total volume is larger than before. The NAC essentially produces no commodities. It is purely a market place where a number of agencies meet to exchange commodities. The NSC, with its large staff and broad jurisdiction, is a producer in its own right. It manufactures advice and position papers, and invents new schemes for foreign policy.

There are a number of interagency committees newer and less well organized than the NAC. The President's Special Trade Representative heads three of these: The Trade Executive Committee, the Trade Staff Committee, and the Trade Information Committee.[3] Representatives are drawn from the departments of State, Treasury, Defense, Commerce, Labor, Agriculture, and Interior. The Treasury considers the STR's committees a major market place. It works aggressively to assert its position here. State, Treasury, Labor, and the STR have a special committee to oversee the U.S.-Canada automotive parts agreement. Another interdepartmental committee was concerned with the balance of payments. This committee met seldom, only three or four times a year. Its main purpose was assembly. It assured that the Treasury was supplied with the data from which it produced the balance of payment statistics.

Task forces are a market place with a shorter life span than other interagency committees. They are organized temporarily to study a particular problem, make recommendations, and then dissolve. Since their recommendations are often far-reaching proposals for reorganization, the agencies being examined are extremely concerned and seek to be represented as strongly as possible.

Some of the interagency committees are secret or semi-secret. The Treasury's Under Secretary for Monetary Affairs chairs such a committee. Neither its jurisdiction nor membership are public.

The Labor Advisory Committee on Foreign Assistance is an example of a market place which includes a major contingent from outside the government. This committee brings representatives from State, Labor, and AID together with representatives from organized labor. AFL-CIO president George Meany chairs the committee. The State Department members include assistant secretaries and labor advisors from the geographic bureaus and representatives of the Labor Office. Labor Department members include the Assistant Secretary for International Labor Affairs and geographic desk officers from the ILAB. AID members include the administrator, and assistant administrators and labor advisors from the geographic bureaus. In addition to "the Honest Plumber" who heads the committee, organized labor is represented by several trade union national presidents and by Jay Lovestone, the AFL-CIO's "Secretary of State."[4]

Interagency bargaining does not always take place in markets as highly structured as these. Many markets are ad hoc. The bargaining will occur at interdepartmental meetings called for a specific issue. Prior to an Intelsat launch, Comsat, as the "chosen instrument of U.S. foreign policy," gets instructions at a meeting of the State Department, the FCC, and the Office of Telecommunications Policy. The State Department represents foreign policy interests. The FCC represents private users' interests and the Telecommunications Office, through the Interdepartmental Radio Advisory Committee, represents government users' interests.

Sometimes a representative of one department is invited to participate informally in the meetings of another department. The State Department invites representatives from Treasury and Labor to attend its staff meetings. State makes it clear that attendance is a privilege and not a right. The visitor must be specifically invited each time. A retired Treasury official said that when he was a regional desk officer the Assistant Secretary of State for that region used to invite him to the bureau's weekly luncheon. Such hospitality, however, is not a commonly reported occurrence.

The labor attaché conferences held in New Delhi and Tunis have been market places. The chief commodities exchanged at them has been information. The Labor Department offers labor information. The State Department offers policy information. The labor attachés give the two departments news from the field and exchange information and techniques among themselves.

Finally, bargaining may take place without any physical market site at all. The market place is the abstract network of interrelationships among the various agencies in the arena. Sometimes the market is neatly defined in an official requirement for clearance. The Munitions Control Act provides that export of articles subject to the Act need the clearance of the Science Bureau and ACDA at the State Department and the offices of International Security Affairs and Research and Engineering at the Department of Defense. Other abstract markets are not so handily circumscribed. The market for the balance of payment not only includes the State Department and the Treasury, but also Commerce, Agriculture, Defense, and the Council of Economic Advisors, to name just a few. When the International Organizations Bureau prepares a speech on space policy for delivery at the United Nations it must clear it with the Science Bureau, the U.S. delegation at New York, and NASA. Import-export matters must be cleared by State's Economic, Legal, and Science Bureaus, and the Treasury's International Office and Bureau of Customs.

Many agencies have established bureaus which specialize in interagency exchange. Within AID, one is the Participating Agency Staff (PAS) of the Office of Procurement. The sole responsibility of the PAS is to administer AID's contracts with other federal departments. The PAS assembles AID's requirements, negotiates interagency agreements, and supervises their implementation. The USAID missions send their requests for services into Washington. A typical request would be for a three month training program at the Bureau of Labor Statistics for a labor ministry statistician.[5] In Washington the AID bureaus evaluate various requests from the missions and forward the consolidated requests to the PAS. The PAS negotiates a contract with the ILAB to furnish this training.

AID contracts follow two forms. First is an individual contract for a specific service. This is known as a PASA, for Participating Agency Service Agreement. Physically a PASA is a five to ten page contract which describes the exact project and how it is to be funded. Personnel, supplies, and technical services are each described on a separate form. It includes the form signed by the foreign government when it requested the aid originally.

The second contract between AID and a participating agency is an annualized budget agreement. This is the aggregation of the individual contracts projected over the coming year. Physically, it is one sheet of budget figures followed by a ten to twenty page general description of the program for the coming year. While the annualized budget agreement is quite specific in the figures it lists, there is actually a great deal of flexibility. The final cost of the PASA is not the sum contracted for originally but the actual cost computed at the end of the year at the rates agreed to. For example, if the Labor Department agrees to send a DOLITAC advisor to Korea for twenty-four months and the man only stays twenty-two months, AID pays for the twenty-two months, not the original twenty-four months. The PAS believes that the participating agencies occasionally overspend because they know that in the end AID will always pay. Still AID does not begrudge them the money since it was its own missions which requested the services in the first place. In training programs the final cost usually falls short of the estimate because of attrition. Many potential trainees cannot be sent to the United States because they are deficient in English or cannot meet the security standards. In the largest training program, that run by the Department of Agriculture, the predeparture attrition is 30 percent. Other agencies do not have such a high rate.

The market for exchange among the agencies studied is tiered in a fashion analogous to the tiering of the economic market into assorted wholesale and retail levels. Interagency exchange must occur at the right level and bargaining must take place at the right level. When it begins at too low a level it cannot be successfully concluded. The issue is too important to be decided on that tier. In this case it is "bucked up" to a higher level where it can be decided. An NAC member noted: "When major political questions are involved, the NAC realizes that there is no point in staffing because it is basically a high level decision. Staffing will be limited to presenting the facts." Another official said "We only trade off small things." Interviewees were aware of the level to which their counterparts in other agencies were allowed to bargain. The State Department is contemptuous of the Treasury because it gives less autonomy to its bargainers. The Treasury insists that many decisions be authorized one or two levels higher than in the State Department. The Treasury will "buck up" the approval of a bargaining position to an assistant secretary when the State Department decides it at a staff level.

Bargaining between NASA and the State Department on the issue of U.S. policy toward the location of a tracking station in the Union of South Africa exemplifies the behavior of the two agencies in the bureaucratic market place. NASA likes the South African location because it is ideally located to track and communicate with spacecraft launched down the Atlantic Range and because the South Africans supply all the funds and technicians to operate the station. The United States supplies only one man, the director formally in charge of the facility. The State Department is ambivalent. The International Organizations Bureau considers the station a liability in United Nations activities. Delegates from the black African nations attack the station as evidence of United States support of the apartheid regime. The African Bureau agrees with this, yet it also likes the contacts it gives with South Africa. American relations with the Union are limited. The tracking station gives an entré in a politically non-sensitive area. The utility of the station is higher than ordinary because other contacts are so few. The station also comes under criticism from congressmen who are opposed to any U.S. support of apartheid. The Science Bureau acts as the middleman between NASA and the State Department bureaus. It explains to the International Organizations Bureau NASA's desire to keep the station and explains to NASA how the station handicaps the U.S. delegation to the United Nations. One result of this bargaining was that when NASA began to search for a site for the 210 foot antenna for tracking and communication with vehicles in deep space, South Africa was assigned a low rating along the political dimension. Partly because of this NASA located the new station in Spain.

NASA, USIA, and the State Department were the chief bargainers in arranging for the world tours of the Apollo 11 and 12 astronauts.[6] The points the three agencies dickered over included the itinerary, funding, and personnel. USIA proposed an itinerary designed to give the astronauts maximum exposure. The State Department wanted them to meet the political leadership in each country. NASA worried that the pace would be too strenuous. In both trips the USIA agreed to cut back the itinerary. Costs were shared by having each agency pay its own personnel per diem. The Air Force, at White House request, furnished a Special Air Mission aircraft. The USIA paid all costs of publicity and public affairs. The embassies provided communication, local transportation, temporary office space, and accommodations. NASA supplied gifts for the astronauts to present to the chiefs of state and other dignitaries at each stop. These gifts were tiny moon rocks, a replica of the plaque left on the moon, a flag returned from the moon, and autographed photographs of lunar activities. Personnel came from NASA's International Office, State's Office of Protocol, and USIA's Office of Policy and Plans. Since the trip was a desirable commodity, the bargaining involved cutting down the number of personnel permitted to accompany the astronauts.

Although the bargaining over these issues of itinerary, costs, and personnel was on a quid pro quo basis, this particular exchange was but one part of the continuing flow of commodities between the three agencies. Some of this more general flow of less specific commodities was manifested in the bargaining meetings. One of the first orders of business when the interagency committees met to plan the trips was to set out the objectives. The three agencies agreed to a four point statement of goals: (1) The trip would tell the story of a great American success achieved through the united effort of thousands of people. (2) Seen from space, the earth is small and fragile. All nations should cooperate to preserve and improve it for all mankind. (3) Space exploration is a scientific program. Its first rewards have been satellites for communication, weather, and earth resources surveying. (4) The space program is expensive. The United States needs the rest of the world to contribute its talent and money.[7]

This statement of goals displays some contribution from each agency. USIA sought to capitalize on the public relations advantage of the astronauts. Adopting conspicuously economic terminology its report of the Apollo 12 tour said "Space is an easily saleable commodity in the market place of ideas." "Space (especially when personified by an astronaut) still provides an entré for USIS and other embassy officers to both media and key government officials, often when approaches on other matters of U.S. concern are difficult or unacceptable," it continued.[8] The State Department concurred with this goal and also sought to emphasize the U.S. dedication to peace. All three agencies liked to emphasize the third point about the practical applications of the science exploration. NASA liked the fourth point which asked for contributions.

These were the benefits the agencies hoped to get. Their inputs were not so evenly balanced. NASA was overwhelmingly the major contributor. It put in the astronauts and their successful moon landing. Neither the State Department nor USIA could offer anything coming close to that commodity. The State Department contributed the arrangements for the trip and USIA contributed its publicity network. Yet because of the varying utilities of each commodity to its contributor, the exchange was possible. The astronauts' presence might have a high utility to the State Department and the USIA but it was not a big sacrifice to NASA. The Apollo program had no need for them for several months. It had a dozen other highly trained astronauts waiting in Houston. The astronauts could do more for the space agency on tour repaying old obligations and earning new credits. The State Department and USIA had a similar variation in utility. Their resources of men and material had a higher utility if they were shifted from their routine duties to enhancing the impact of the astronauts. The tour gave the diplomats access which they had otherwise lacked. In Dar es Salaam President Nyerere had resisted the embassy's overtures to introduce television to his country. He feared that it would feed his people's revolution of rising expectations. Yet when the Apollo 12 astronauts told him about the educational television satellite program with India, he said it might be a good innovation for Tanzania.[9] The tour had opened a new political point of approach for the embassy.

The market place for bargaining between the State Department and the Treasury on economic issues differs from bargaining in the space market place insofar as the protagonists share the same background. This was not true in the space arena. The economic issue bargainers are likely to be trained economists on both sides. In the space arena it is the scientists versus the diplomats. One FSO who deals in financial matters commented, "We are all professional economists so we share the same approach with the Treasury." However, the shared professionalism has a reverse side. Since neither side has an exclusive expertise, one does not defer to the knowledge of the other. The NASA scientist did not challenge the diplomat nor did the diplomat challenge the scientist. But the economists of the Treasury and the State Department are constantly challenging each other. Bargaining between the two departments is marked by greater strife. Respondents frequently used the vocabulary of warfare. "We are the ones who fight the border tax question." When asked about the Treasury one FSO snapped, "They are the enemy." Another referred to his counterparts as "a bunch of bandits."

Policy toward the underdeveloped nations is one area of conflict in bargaining. Beginning with the Marshall Plan in 1947 the State Department has traditionally favored more foreign aid while the Treasury has opposed it. This ties in with their respective constituencies. The State Department's clientele is the foreign nations with which it conducts diplomacy. It is oriented toward their needs. In the words of one of its Treasury critics, it wants to "spend, spend, spend." The Treasury has a different constituency. Its clientele is financially conservative bankers and businessmen. Like the State Department it too has foreign clients but these, the foreign financial ministries and central banks, are equally conservative.

This opposing orientation arose in bargaining between the State Department and the Treasury on the establishment of the system of Special Drawing Rights. The Special Drawing Rights are the "paper gold" created by the International Monetary Fund in 1969.[10] The SDRs are bank credits which may be used in lieu of gold or capital currencies as reserve funds. Their adoption came after a long struggle to overcome the distrust of ultraconservative European bankers. Through them the IMF hopes to overcome the liquidity crisis which has plagued the international monetary system since the 1950s. The State Department proposed to study the use of the SDRs to extend aid to the underdeveloped nations. SDRs are ideally suitable for this purpose since they are designed to create new capital. Giving a few SDRs to an underdeveloped nation would give it a modest endowment with which to begin economic expansion. The Treasury strongly opposed this idea. It considered the SDR system to be in a delicate infancy. A foolish plan like this could undermine confidence in the SDRs and ruin years of careful negotiating. The Treasury refused to consider the proposal. The State Department would at least like to study it.

The two departments have divergent views on the border tax issue. Both agree that American exporters labor under a tax handicap. GATT allows rebate of the value added taxes of the European countries but not of the corporate income tax in the United States. But the two departments do not agree on how to remedy the situation. The Treasury takes a hard line. It wants to change the GATT rules. It does not care whether the proposed change is negotiable internationally. The State Department is interested in the international effects. It must have a position which is negotiable. It is concerned with preserving the system to assure stability. It believes that any American proposal must be equitable. The current result of the bargaining seems to please both departments. It is the Domestic International Sales Corporation (DISC) mentioned in chapter 2. With corporation income tax rates of 50 percent the DISC would offer major savings to exporters. The Treasury likes this. The DISC seems to be legal under the GATT. The State Department likes this. Thus the Treasury receives permission to proceed with a device for improving the balance of payments while the State Department receives concessions that make the program acceptable internationally.

In relating these specific examples of bargaining the officials interviewed mentioned a number of rules of strategy. These rules fall into two sets: rules of consensus and rules of conflict. The first set resembled the maxims of politics: find common interests; find allies; build coalitions. The second set resembled the maxims of the military: knows the terrain; occupy key positions; keep reinforcements close by; defeat the enemy.

In terms of economic exchange theory the two sets of rules correspond to a bargainer's location off or on the Paretian optimum. Welfare economists explain the Paretian optimum by means of an Edgeworth box (see figure 6-1). This is a diagram named for Francis Ysidro Edgeworth who first suggested it in 1881.[11] To explain the bargaining situation, Edgeworth took two utility

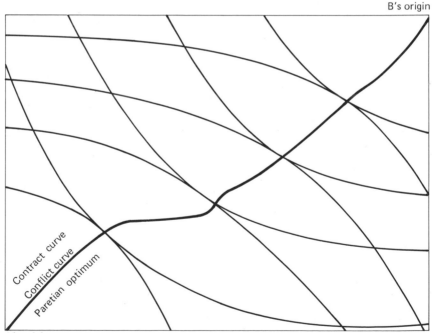

Figure 6-1. Edgeworth Box.

maps, one for each party. Each map shows the bargainer's preferences between two commodities (X and Y). Since the two bargainers (A and B) are opposed, he opposed the two utility maps so that they overlapped. This gives a series of football shaped ovals oriented on a northwest-southeast axis. Each oval represents the "bargaining space" between the two parties. A's origin is in the lower left corner. Moving generally to the northeast he reaches increasingly desirable indifference curves. B's origin is in the opposite corner, at the upper right. Since his map has been reversed he reaches increasingly more desirable indifference curves by moving southwest. Because each party is indifferent between points on the same indifference curve, each is perfectly willing to slide along his curve. But as he slides along his indifference curve, the other party moves to a higher or lower indifference curve of his own. That is, as A is moving from one point to another which is equally desirable to him, B is either moving to a point he prefers more or less than the original point. Thus B can improve his situation while A's situation remains the same or he can worsen his situation while A's remains the same. Of course there is no reason A has to slide along the same indifference curve. Both A and B can be shifting curves at the same time. Both can be improving their circumstances at once. In other words, they have common interests. Their common interests are shown on the diagram as their bargaining space, the football shaped oval just described. This joint improvement increases until they reach a point where they no longer have common interests. Their indifference curves are tangent. No bargaining space remains. Depending on where they started and their bargaining path, this point where their common interests ends is on a curve running from A's origin to B's origin. Economists have several names for this curve. They call it the contract curve because it traces the points where bargaining reaches an end. The joint profits of the exchange have been maximized; the terms of the exchange are agreed upon. They call it the conflict curve because movement along the line can only profit one party at the expense of the other. Since the greatest joint profit has been achieved one party can only move to a higher indifference curve by forcing the other to a lower one. They also call this curve the Paretian optimum in honor of Vilfredo Pareto, the Italian economist who developed the concept of optimality.[12]

The Edgeworth box gives two sets of points: first are those not on the conflict curve. These are sub-optimal. Bargaining space remains. Second are those on the conflict curve. All advantages have been optimized. Neither party can improve his position without worsening that of the other. Movement along the curve will improve the situation of one only at the expense of the other. Movement off the curve may worsen the positions of both.

These two sets of points in the Edgeworth box correspond to the two types of bargaining situations: consensus and conflict. The first set of sub-optimal points corresponds to the consensus situation. Because bargaining space remains, the bargainers can continue to find common interests. The first set of political rules of strategy are appropriate here. The bargaining milieu tends to be relaxed.

The negotiations between the ILAB and AID follows this first pattern. Each party comes to the meeting to decide the level of the annual budget agreement armed with his own sheaves of figures. AID computes its estimates for the requests it has received from its missions overseas. The ILAB computes its estimates from reports by the labor attaché. The two sets of estimates match fairly closely since they are supposed to have been coordinated at the embassy level. But even if the estimates diverge the two sides are not particularly concerned. They both realize that there will be many further adjustments during the year. Not all foreign trainees will arrive. Not all DOLITAC advisors will depart. Some projects will be cancelled. Others will be added. The two agencies recognize that they are so far out from the conflict curve that plenty of bargaining space remains. The application of one AID contractual provision serves as a clear example of the aid agency's willingness to slide along its indifference curve while the Labor Department moves to a higher one. The standard annual budget agreement states that funds assigned to one of the participating agency's bureaus may not be shifted to another bureau without AID's permission.[13] Actually AID is quite willing to allow a participating agency to shift funds between its bureaus if it wishes to. AID's approval is, in the words of one of its staff, "strictly *pro forma*."

The Treasury places greater emphasis on consensus in bargaining than the other departments. "We reach consensus ninety-nine times out of a hundred" said one official referring to the NAC meetings. One technique of fostering consensus is to discourage early closure on a policy. "Agencies come to the meetings with rather tentative views." If agencies disagree the NAC suspends consideration of that issue. Either the two agencies "work it out between themselves" or the issue is "kicked upstairs." The members defer to the agency most responsible. The benefit of the doubt goes to the institution proposing the transaction. The source of the funds is a key factor. Lending institutions get more autonomy the less dependent they are on congressionally appropriated money. The NAC seldom interferes with the wealthy and self-sufficient World Bank. Within the NAC the Treasury seeks to enhance consensus. "The Treasury is the balancing wheel," said a Treasury respondent after describing how the other agencies all sought to advance their own interests.

A veto is a vote specifically designed to assure consensus. All veto-holders must agree before action can occur; one objection will end the proposal. The NAC is aware of this and accordingly uses its right to veto financial transactions cautiously. Rather than veto a transaction about which it has qualms, the NAC will let it go through but will threaten to veto any future transactions of the same type. Other times when its vote is necessary for approval it will withhold its vote as a polite veto.

The clearance system whereby position papers are routed to a series of offices for approval gives each an opportunity to veto. The system forces consensus. On one hand, it assures that all agree on a policy position. On the other, to disapprove a paper requires good nerves and a strong argument. Said one FSO, "You can easily be overruled." Another said "A good bureaucratic solution is to make your point as strongly as possible and then relax." In this he recognized both the need for consensus and his limited power to force his will on the group even were he willing to go to any extreme.

FSOs put great emphasis on consensus. The shibboleth in their jargon is "the team." Labor attachés and Treasury representatives should get on the embassy team. For the FSO this sort of consensus is a weapon to be used to discipline the improperly socialized attachés or the wayward economists in their midst. This concept of consensus does not necessarily leave bargaining space. At times the only common interest appears to be that of not embarrassing the U.S. government.

The final rule of bargaining strategy falling in the consensus set is that of vagueness. Parties in a bargaining situation often find it easier to agree on a vague position than on an exact one. Exact proposals contain many awkward disadvantages; vague ones, only glorious advantages. One FSO recommends presenting a new idea orally rather than in writing. He claims that he has much greater success that way. By outlining his idea in a vague way he preserves a larger bargaining space. His listeners can each imagine their own preferred location within the space. A more specific proposal would cut away at the amount of bargaining space. It would move both parties closer to the conflict curve.

Once the bargaining space is gone, and the parties reach the conflict curve, the situation changes radically. The atmosphere shifts from consensus to conflict. Bargaining strategy shifts from political to military. The first rule in this set is know the enemy. Good intelligence is a necessity. Learn his order of battle, how the various bureaus stand on the issue. Sound him out early. Ask a senior bureaucrat what the other agency's probable disposition and course of action will be. The Treasury gets informal advance warnings of proposed transactions of the international institution before the NAC receives the official notification.

If the bureaucratic intelligence reports indicate conflict is in the offing, the next rule is careful preparation. A policy should be developed fully if it is likely to come under attack at an early juncture. One FSO recommended: "If your idea is likely to be killed in the embryonic stages, wait until it grows into a lusty child before exposing it."

When the bureaucratic intelligence network discovers a threat from another agency, the best defense is to quash it in the early stages. "We try to nip these things in the bud," explained an interviewee. Once a proposal reaches the stage of consideration at a formal interagency meeting it is hard to stop. Its proponents are committed to it and find it hard to back down. Stopping a proposal early avoids this problem.

When conflict escalates into an all-out battle the two keys to victory are position and movement. Advantages go to the side that can determine the rules of the battle. One Treasury official complained that the State Department wants to play by a diplomatic set of rules whereas the domestic agencies want to play by "American" rules. Diplomatic rules provide for indirect bargaining. The bargainers discuss the issue at a cocktail party. The value of information is based on the status of its source. A fact has more weight if it comes from an assistant secretary than if it comes from a GS 14. Knowledge learned from experience is more valued than that from analysis.[14] American rules are direct. When one official wants to bargain he picks up the telephone and calls his opposite number. Information is valued according to its merit rather than its source. Neither hierarchy nor experience has a monopoly on truth. The Treasury objects to the un-American diplomatic rules. It wants to play by its own rules.

In the relationships studied, a second way to gain an advantageous bureaucratic position is to control the agenda. The agency which determines the issues has a major advantage. The corollary to this is to be the chairman of the meeting. More than the other agencies studied, the State Department favors this technique of controlling the chair in interagency meetings. It tries to see that such a provision is written into new legislation. Other times it relies on its traditional right to primacy in foreign affairs.

The physical site of the bargaining is significant. Hosting a bargaining session confers a strategic advantage on the sponsor. The Labor Department, the most disadvantaged of the four agencies, nearly always goes to Foggy Bottom for meetings. NASA and the State Department reciprocate evenly. The Treasury sponsors the meetings on financial issues. By channeling all interagency bargaining through one office, the Participating Agency Staff, AID is able to enhance its control of the site. The PAS keeps all the files. It has the relevant information readily accessible. It prints the forms for the PASAs and the annual budget agreement. With these inducements it lures the participating agency over to its Thomas Circle building for the negotiating sessions.

The fourth strategic rule of position is that of rigidity. It is the same as the military maxim of burning one's bridges behind him. If there is no avenue of retreat, the troops must defend their position successfully. If an agency has no other option remaining, then the other agency must accept its proposal. Technical rigidity is the best kind. NASA has the edge here. If NASA must have a tracking station in South Africa because it is in the path of launch from Cape Kennedy, then the State Department can do little to change it. If NASA needs deep space tracking stations in boxes 120 degrees apart and just outside the path of flight, then the State Department has only a few countries to choose among. The Treasury can also benefit from its technical rigidity. It has on occasion declared that the balance of payments situation was so unfavorable that the State Department had to take action. Other times it has purposely placed itself in positions of rigidity by entering into conditional international agreements whereby U.S. action is a prerequisite for action by other parties to the agreement. Often an American contribution is needed to "trigger" contributions from other donors. This was the line of argument followed by the Secretary of the Treasury in 1968 in presenting his brief for replenishment of the International

Development Association. Adopting the position that the United States had no choice the secretary warned that:

If the United States were to fail to contribute its 40-percent share of the proposed increase in IDA resources, the entire proposal, involving contributions by 18 other developed countries who are putting up more than we are, would collapse, and the vital work of this institution would come to a complete halt. It is not in our interest to let this happen.[15]

The amount of Public Law 480 funds available is computed according to an inflexible formula. When the Treasury tells the Labor Department how many rupees are available in counterpart funds, the Labor Department cannot ask for a little more because it had planned a bigger program for India. The labor attaché program has been more vulnerable to the Johnson and Nixon personnel cutbacks than the rest of the Foreign Service because the majority of the labor attachés hold reserve rather than regular commissions. FSRs lack the job protection of FSOs. When the reduction is ordered the FSOs cannot be dismissed, so the FSRs bear the brunt.

The other key element in battle strategy is movement. It is equally as important as position. The first rule of movement is to seize the initiative. On the bureaucratic battlefield victory often goes to the first down on paper. The first position paper drafted usually has the best chance of being adopted. Even when it is not adopted it at least frames the issues. If a bureau fails to gain the initiative, it may be able to compensate with quantity. Gordon Tullock relates the story of an FSO in the Bureau of Intelligence and Research who wrote a fourteen page paper trenchantly analyzing a diplomatic problem. But no one would read it. So the author ordered all his subordinates to write reports developing various aspects. He stapled all the reports together, retitled his "Introduction and Summary," and put it at the front. He then circulated the entire hundred-fifty page tome among his superiors. They all read only his "Summary" and commended him highly.[16]

The second rule of movement is to outflank the opponent. If one bureau staunchly opposes a proposal, find a way to implement it without going through that bureau. Pockets of resistance should be bypassed. Moving to a different level in the hierarchy can bypass a stubborn opponent. A favorite end run is to discover new legislation allowing a project or to invent a new scheme within the constraints of the old legislation.

Surprise can carry the day. A thoroughly prepared proposal may speed through an interagency meeting chiefly because no one is organized to oppose it. While surprise is considered good strategy in interagency bargaining, deception clearly is not. Time after time the officials questioned on this stressed that trickery was counter-productive. Deceit is not outlawed; many related cases where they had tried it. It was just poor strategy. The party deceived would retaliate at a later date. A good reputation is more valuable than any temporary gain from sneakiness.

7 Production

Production, whether it occurs in the foreign policy bureaucracy or the automobile industry, is the process of increasing the value of a commodity.[1] Manufacturing is an obvious example. A mining company mines iron ore which it sells to the steel mill. The steel mill smelts the ore into steel ingots. The rolling mill rolls the ingots into sheet. The automobile company stamps the sheet into parts and assembles the parts into an automobile. Each of these steps in manufacturing is production. Each increases the value of the original commodity. This sort of manufacturing is descriptive of the assembly and refining of bureaucratic commodities of Group 2 (assembled) and Group 3 (refined).

Yet a commodity does not necessarily have to be physically transformed in order to be productive.[2] Transportation is productive. Shipping the iron ore to the steel mill increases its value. So does shipping the automobile from the assembly line to the dealer. Making the commodity available to the consumer is productive. The new car dealer is productive because he makes the commodity accessible to the consumer by offering an individual item, providing information about it, and arranging financing, all at a convenient location. This productivity of transportation and brokerage is found in conjunction with the basic commodities of Group 1.

Finally, there is the productivity of innovation. In the automobile industry this involves engineering and design. In the bureaucracy this involves Group 4 (invented) commodities.

Brokerage

Brokerage is the function of bringing the supplier and the demander together to make an exchange.[3] A broker may be distinguished from other middlemen who go beyond simply bringing the two parties together. The broker does not add any input of his own. He takes market forces where he finds them. A bureaucratic broker generally deals in Group 1 commodities. As he becomes more involved in assembling, refining, or inventing commodities, he becomes less of a broker. Of course, these various divisions are arbitrary and blend into each other.

A broker makes a market. He brings the two parties to an exchange together, either physically or, more likely, functionally. Indeed the easier it is for the parties to come together, the less need they will have for the broker's services. Thus, well developed markets will be less likely to have as many personnel engaged in brokerage. The most basic service of a broker is to search out offers and bids, then to match the two. This involves having good knowledge of both sides of an exchange. It is a matter of information, not substantive information, but information pertaining to current resources and the demands for these resources.[4]

Certain offices tend to specialize in brokerage. Since these offices are small, this is often tantamount to saying certain officers specialize in brokerage. The ILAB is the chief location on the Labor Department side for those engaged in brokerage between Labor and State. The first of those brokers is the Assistant to the Administrator (Foreign Service). This liaison officer is responsible for the personnel aspects of the State-Labor relations. He deals with the selection, promotion and assignment of labor attachés. He sits on some of the interagency panels and recommends who should sit on the others. A current issue is the threatened cutback in the number of labor attachés posts. Operation Reduction is hitting the labor attaché program particularly hard. The number of labor attachés has been cut from sixty-seven to fifty-two.[5] The State Department views the labor attaché position as an easy place to cut and is proceeding to do so. The Labor Department naturally does not want any cuts, but if they must come it has certain priorities as to which posts should be cut. The ILAB's Foreign Service liaison officer must mediate between the two positions.

The second brokerage center is in the Office of Country Programs. This office includes the five geographic area specialists. Each of these area specialists serves as a link to the corresponding geographic bureau at the State Department. In comparison with the Foreign Service liaison officer, the area specialists tend to contribute less of their own input. In this sense they are purer brokers. They take the market forces where they find them and try to bring the two parties together on this basis. The Foreign Service liaison officer tends to assert his own position more, thereby being less of a pure broker.

The ILAB's third broker is the Office of Program Development and Coordination, which includes the Division of International Technical Assistance. This office deals with AID. It administers the DOLITAC program and the PASAs. The Program Office is a good example of straight brokerage. It contributes little of its own. Rather it works entirely to fit Labor Department resources to AID demands. AID annually sends the Program Office a list of its requests for advisors to go overseas during the coming year. The Program Office matches these to the manpower it has available in the DOLITAC corps. When no DOLITACer is available, the Program Office tries to locate a suitable candidate elsewhere in the Labor Department who would like to serve and who is eligible for the DOLITAC Reserve. The actual negotiations between the Program Office and AID focus on the issues of price. What is to be the DOLITACer's rank? How much will AID transfer to the Labor Department for compensation? This is a fairly pure form of brokerage. It consists only of seeking out the bids and offers, then matching the two.

In its dealings with the Labor Department, the State Department's chief brokerage centers are the Office of Labor Affairs and the five labor advisors in geographic bureaus. The Labor Office is technically in AID but serves the regular State Department as well. As mentioned in chapter 2 the director serves a concurrent role as the Secretary of State's Special Assistant for International Labor Affairs. The Labor Office is particularly concerned with the operation of the labor attaché program. The Office closely follows the attachés careers and the conduct of the program. A major concern is filling key posts.

The State Department's five geographic bureaus each have a labor advisor who is responsible for overseeing the labor aspects of the diplomatic effort in the countries within his region. Basically this resolves itself into being a broker. A geographic bureau labor advisor interviewed said that his job was to "interpret one department to the other." The geographic bureau staff would ask him what the Labor Department policy was with respect to a certain issue. "There was no expertise in this. I knew both ends and brought the ends together." Other times bringing the ends together consisted of arranging meetings. Often these would include trade union leaders. He arranged for Mennen "Soapy" Williams to meet George Meany. Another time he brought Meany together with the ambassador to South Africa to discuss the American policy toward that country's policy of apartheid. On still another occasion this labor advisor arranged for his own bureau's assistant secretary to address a national meeting of the editors of labor newspapers. For the most part, however, the broker deals in the more mundane commodities of cables, reports, and statistics. Indeed certain commodities are beyond this jurisdiction. One noted, for example, that while he can negotiate for the delivery of a speech by an assistant secretary, he cannot handle one by the Secretary of State. "If the AFL-CIO wanted Rogers to speak, they would go to Phil Delaney." He also noted that when in the 1950s the United Auto Workers wanted the United States to boycott South African gold as a sanction against apartheid, the UAW delegation went directly to Secretary Dulles.

Within AID, the Participating Agency Staff (PAS) described in chapter 6 acts as a broker in the aid agency's dealings with the Labor Department. It negotiates with the ILAB's Program Office. The PAS is an even better example of a straight brokerage function than the Program Office. AID has chosen to centralize all the negotiations with participating agencies in this one staff. The PAS handles seventeen separate programs, each with a different department or agency. One result of this centralization is that the PAS's interests tend to be divorced from the interests of the operating divisions which are requesting the services. To counteract some of the disadvantages of this system a representative of the AID bureau whose program is being discussed will participate in the negotiations. When the program involves training foreign labor ministry officials at the Bureau of Labor Statistics, a representative from AID's Office of International Training will participate. When it involves a DOLITAC assignment overseas, a representative from the appropriate country desk will attend.

As befits a centralized administrative division, the PAS is more concerned with management standards than the substantive program. One index it uses to measure managerial efficiency is the ratio of instructors to trainees. One training program may have ten students for each instructor whereas another may have a twenty-five to one ratio. When the PAS uncovers anomalies of this sort it investigates. The staff does not have a rigid ratio that it enforces. The first curriculum may require more instructors, while a second requires fewer. Nevertheless the PAS uses efficiency indices such as this as a starting point for evaluating management standards. This concern with efficiency marks and the PAS as highly specialized in brokerage. Consolidation of AID's negotiations with the participating agencies has extended the market (to use Adam Smith's phrase) to the point where such specialization has become possible.

The pattern of specialization in brokerage within NASA follows the pattern found in the Labor Department. In that department the bureaucratic brokers dealing with the State Department were found in the ILAB. Similarly in NASA the brokers are in the Office of International Affairs. And, again the same pattern, the brokerage function is found concentrated in a few individuals.

The first of these is the International Organization Director. As his title implies he and his small staff serve as brokers between NASA and the State Department's International Organization Bureau. Their chief concern is the U.N. Committee on the Peaceful Uses of Outer Space. The director meets frequently with State's International Organization Bureau and the American delegation in New York. Between meetings the brokerage continues over the telephone and in memorandums. The director sees his role to be that of bringing NASA's technical input together with the State Department's political input. NASA is continually generating new commodities. Many of these are of the Group 4 category. In order for these invented commodities to be utilized, channels must be found to bring them to bear on practical applications. The State Department offers access to some of these channels in the form of international treaties. For example, NASA has a potential for rescuing Soviet cosmonauts trapped in orbit (and vice versa) but this potential can only be realized if the two countries can standardize some of their equipment. The State Department has access to the Soviets at the U.N. Space Committee, but in order to benefit from State's access NASA has to get its own access to the State Department. This is done through the International Organization Director. The State Department's International Organizations Bureau is interested in utilizing the Space Committee as a way to strengthen the United Nations; NASA is interested in rescuing astronauts. The NASA International Organization Director brings the two together.

The second broker in NASA's International Office is the Operations Support Director. His chief contact point at Foggy Bottom is the Science Bureau. His interest is in the support of foreign nations for the NASA program. Tracking stations are one of his major responsibilities. In a typical sequence the Office of Tracking and Data Acquisition would tell the Support Director that a new site was needed. It would give the general area. Next the Support Director would discuss this with State's Science Bureau. Together they would select several tentative sites. After the embassy secured permission from the host country, NASA's Tracking Office would send a survey team to thoroughly evaluate these tentative sites. Once the survey team had decided which site or sites it wanted, the responsibility would shift back to the State Department for the final negotiation of the cooperative agreement between the embassy and the host country's foreign ministry. The Support Director perceived his role as one of brokerage in his own description of his duties: "We are an interface between the technical and the non-technical. We translate technical information into non-technical." The issues which concern the State Department take a considerably different form from those which concern the Tracking Office. The State Department's concerns are a projection of the concerns of the potential host country. The State Department wants to know: How many American personnel will be employed at the tracking station? How many years will they stay? How much land will be needed? How much money will be spent in the local economy?

A third broker in NASA's International Office is the Special Assistant for Cooperative Projects. In contrast to the Support division which was concerned with the U.S. program, the cooperative projects division is interested in bilateral or multilateral programs. As of 1970 NASA had entered into agreements with twenty-five foreign countries for cooperative projects. The Alouette I launched jointly with Canada investigated electron density in the ionosphere. The San Marco series with Italy measured the local density of the equitorial upper atmosphere. The Helios project with Germany scheduled for launching in 1974-75 will send a space vehicle close to the sun for a series of nine simultaneous investigations.[6]

The Science Bureau is the State Department's primary brokerage point in dealing with NASA. The FSOs interviewed perceived their role as such. Indeed one respondent spontaneously used the term broker: "We act as a broker between NASA and State." Later he added that "we can act as a broker in finding compromise in cases of conflict because we understand both sides." The broker has an overview of both sides of a given question. As an example, the FSO mentioned the recent preparation of a policy paper for the White House. The State Department geographic bureau took one position while NASA took another. The Science Bureau took a third position between the two. From here, it was able to negotiate a compromise.

Within the State Department the Science Bureau will be dealing either with one of the bureaus in Washington or with an embassy in the field. The embassies are fairly autonomous. They must be persuaded of the merits of a project even when the geographic bureau to which they are officially subordinate has already accepted a NASA proposal. The country desks, as well as the Science Bureau, function as brokers. The Science Bureau's brokerage role may include resolving conflicts between State Department bureaus at the same time as it is bringing in

NASA programs. For example, the recurring issue of technical cooperation with the Union of South Africa includes built-in tension between the African Bureau and the International Organizations Bureau.

The State Department's second major broker in dealing with NASA is the International Organizations Bureau's United Nations Office. The U.N. Office is the link between NASA and the U.N. Space Committee. The State Department has jealously guarded its prerogatives with respect to the Space Committee. It has chosen to treat it very much as a political organization rather than as a technical body. Representation to the main committee is from the regular diplomatic delegation to the United Nations. It is only at the sub-committee level that it allows NASA a leading role. Even here NASA freedom of action is limited. A NASA official heads the delegation only to the sub-committee which is concerned with the technical issues. This delegation chief is still under the "policy guidance" of the State Department, from which he must await instructions.

An FSO in the U.N. Office noted that the commodities he dealt in were information and political support. "I am constantly on the lookout for good ideas from other people." U.N. meetings are a fertile ground from which to gather new ideas. Referring to the second commodity he said "I may have more support for a project in NASA than in my own office." In both of these he displayed a typical brokerage role of searching out the bids and offers and bringing the two parties together. The U.N. Space Committee had some information which NASA wanted. The broker passed it on. The delegation in New York needed some political support on a position which was not forthcoming from Foggy Bottom. The broker found and mobilized this support at NASA.

Timing is an important service of brokerage. The broker can be a memory bank with unaccepted bids and offers of the past stored away to be retrieved when a match is found. An FSO said that he often revived ideas that had been proposed to the U.N. Space Committee in previous years, but had failed because the time was not then right.

The State Department's U.N. Office's relation with NASA is not always smooth. The space agency is not eager to deal through the United Nations. It prefers to operate bilaterally. Bilateral programs are easier to manage since there are only two parties. It is easier to find common ground. There are fewer points of coordination. The emphasis is technical. Political considerations seldom enter. Multilateral U.N. projects lack the simplicity of bilateral arrangements. Each party has its own set of objectives. Furthermore, U.N. projects tend to get politicized. The technical discussion gives way to foreign policy posturing. In bilateral projects the parties tend to bargain according to the amount of money and expertise they are contributing. In U.N. projects the parties tend to bargain according to their political strength in the General Assembly. State's U.N. Office admits these difficulties but supports space cooperation within the framework of the United Nations as part of the overall American policy of supporting the U.N.

Since NASA is often reluctant to engage in U.N. projects State's U.N. Office finds that it must become less of a pure broker and more of a salesman to persuade the space agency to participate. In its sales pitch the U.N. Office points out that NASA needs clientele support and that its potential clientele is world wide. NASA needs access to all parts of the globe. It needs the support of the international scientific community. This recognition of NASA dependence on foreign nations and its vulnerability was summed up by one space official when he said: "NASA wants a climate of open-mindedness and acceptance of space technology. It wouldn't be helpful if an irrational view of the new should prevail." He continued: "NASA wants freedom to experiment. It is a great aid to running a space program if you have international cooperation."

The pattern of specialization in brokerage in the Treasury follows that of the other two domestic agencies, but with important differences in emphasis. Like the Labor Department and NASA, the Treasury concentrates its brokerage functions with the State Department in its International Affairs branch. Again in the same pattern the function is concentrated in a few individuals. But unlike the other two domestic agencies, the Treasury brokers are less willing to accept a passive role of searching out bids and offers and bringing the two together. They are less willing to accept market forces where they are. One effect is that they try to shape the market forces. Another effect is that they just disregard the possibilities of brokerage entirely. They refuse to enter into exchange at all.

The Treasury brokers who most resemble their counterparts in the other agencies are the geographic desk officers. In a rare violation of the orthodox fivefold division of the world, the Treasury desk officers are organized along economic lines. The first is concerned with industrial nations; the second, with developing nations; and the third, with the Alliance for Progress in Latin America. This last category is compatible with the merged State-AID Latin American Bureau, established to promote the Alliance. Each of the three geographic desk officers deals directly with the State Department country desk officers according to the specific problem with which he is concerned. This follows the pattern in the ILAB where the geographic desk officers dealt with the State Department geographic bureaus. In labor affairs, however, the pattern was more orderly. Each geographic bureau had a labor advisor. Economics is not so neatly structured. While each bureau has at least one regional economic officer, his title and importance vary considerably. The Latin American bureau has a large staff devoted to economics. The African Bureau has only a single advisor.

The most broker-like of the Treasury officials is the Director of the Office of International Financial Policy Coordination and Operations when he assumes his alter-ego as Secretary of the National Advisory Committee on International Monetary and Financial Policies. As such he is the mediator of an interdepartmental committee including representatives from the Treasury, the State Department, and seven other departments or organizations. He must maintain strict neutrality. He is not serving on the committee as a Treasury delegate; the Treasury has other men to do that. His job is to promote the smooth functioning of the NAC. All brokers trade in certain commodities. For the NAC Secretary the commodity is votes. He spends his days on the telephone with the various members soliciting their votes. As each issue comes up the secretary makes his telephone rounds sounding out each member's opinion. By the time the weekly meeting comes, he has, hopefully, brought the members into agreement. If not, there is more discussion and compromise at the meeting. Since it is a face to face encounter, the weekly NAC meeting is more like a commercial market than most found in the bureaucracy. In a regular market like this there is less need for a broker. A broker makes the market by bringing the bids and offers together functionally. But when they are brought together physically the buyers and sellers no longer need the broker. The NAC Secretary is less of a broker and more of a sergeant at arms. While this characterization is an exaggerated diminution of the NAC Secretary's role, it does serve to illustrate that by structuring the international financial policy market more, less brokerage is necessary.

A number of the other offices within the International Affairs branch engage in brokerage. These cover trade, the balance of payments, gold, foreign currencies, and statistics. Each area has its own brokerage channels to the State Department.

While the Treasury does have a system of brokerage channels with the State Department, the network is much smaller than it could be. The Treasury will disregard and even rebuff State Department bids and offers for exchange. Whereas the Labor Department and NASA will be eager to enter into negotiations with the State Department, the Treasury holds itself aloof. At times it will even appear hostile to State Department overtures. In part this seems to be the product of the Treasury's successful invasion of the State Department's bureaucratic jurisdiction. The Treasury has wrested away certain sectors of the foreign affairs territory. Since the Treasury already has free access to this jurisdiction, it has no need to apply to the State Department for a license to operate in its arena. Hence there is no need to bargain.

On the State Department side relations with the Treasury, such as they are, center in two places. First is the geographic bureaus just mentioned. Of these the European Bureau has the most intercourse with the Treasury. There are more economists assigned to the Latin American Bureau, but the Treasury has little interest in this area. Neither department has much interest in the economics of Africa, the Near East, or Asia.

Within the European Bureau is the Office of OECD, European Community, and Atlantic Political-Economic Affairs. The interest of this office and the Treasury coincide closely. Yet while the interests match, the State Department office is overwhelmed by the superior manpower and expertise that the Treasury concentrates in this area. The Department has little to offer the Treasury in an exchange. An FSO lamented that incoming cables were the only commodity in which the European Bureau had a comparative advantage: "The telegraph key—this is the only thing we have a hold of." The Treasury even gets the cables soon after they arrive. Since the European Bureau has little to offer there is little brokerage in the pattern of the other agencies. From the European Bureau's viewpoint it does have something to offer the Treasury, but the Treasury does not want to buy this commodity, which is advice on the political complexities of European economics. The Treasury is technically oriented. It often ignores the political implications of its policies. Treasury policies may offend the European nations, producing backlash. The complaints come to the State Department which earns little sympathy when it forwards them to the Treasury. The State Department's second and more extensive point of contact with the Treasury is its Economic Bureau. Within this bureau the International Finance and Development branch is the one most frequently involved with the Treasury. The FSOs interviewed from this branch saw their role as brokerage, or in their words "coordination" or "liaison." Referring to the various agencies and offices with which he dealt, one economist said "The purpose of this office is to keep them from talking past each other." A different FSO from the same branch estimated that he spent nearly half of his time dealing with the Treasury and another quarter of his time dealing with other departments and agencies outside the State Department. In conducting this brokerage his first problem was to reach agreement within the State Department on a particular policy. This is easier to do in finance than in trade policy because the State Department is more willing to defer to the Treasury in finance. Here the State Department confines its involvement to assuring that the Treasury stays within certain limits. These are chiefly defined by the existing treaty obligations. "Our role has been one of drawing foreign policy limitations." Later he added, "We promote the GATT position." Since the State Department has modest goals in financial policy it is easier to reach consensus internally than in trade policy to which it attaches more importance.

Still the State Department does not entirely confine itself to reminding the Treasury that it must not violate international treaties. It has certain policy positions of its own to promote. One is a concern for the underdeveloped countries. State tries to head off policies which would hurt these nations. It has opposed restrictions on American investment abroad. The Treasury sought the restrictions to help stem the gold outflow. The State Department secured modifications so that the restrictions would have a less deleterious effect on the underdeveloped nations. The State Department also defended these nations in the preparation of a position paper for a Working Party 3 meeting. The Treasury had ignored the relationship between the underdeveloped areas and Europe. The State Department tried to point out that the Europeans were being too greedy. European integration is a second policy the State Department seeks to promote. To this end the State Department has tried to encourage the development of internal European currency "swap lines." A country whose currency was under pressure would get loans from within Europe rather than coming to the United States for the money.

In the trade field the State Department is more assertive and the Treasury is less so. The State Department's more assertive position, however, does not have much effect on brokerage. The Economic Bureau's Trade branch operates much the same as the Finance branch in its dealing with the Treasury. The Trade branch frequently serves as a broker between the country desks and the Treasury; yet at other times the desks will go directly to the Office of Industrial Nations or some other appropriate geographic desk at the Treasury. An FSO from the Trade branch noted that there was little conflict between State and Treasury. There tended to be more conflict between State and Commerce or State and Agriculture. He attributed this to a clear demarcation of the spheres of influence between State and Treasury in trade matters.

One aspect of the spheres of influence is that there is less exchange between the two departments. The bureaucratic border can be kept more peaceful if there is less activity along it. A lower level of exchange is possible when the State Department can obtain internally what it would otherwise have to obtain from the Treasury. Thus the State Department duplicates certain services of economic analysis which it might have acquired from the Treasury. The Economic Bureau will conduct economic studies itself rather than going outside the department for them. Since both departments have the basic data, the Economic Bureau finds it easier to conduct the study internally than to go to the Treasury. In a move toward bureaucratic autarky the Economic Bureau is establishing a computer data bank and set of programs to manipulate the data.

Assemblage

The productivity of assembling Group 2 commodities is more easily apparent than the productivity of brokerage. Yet in both cases the activity is productive because it increases the value of the commodity, in the first instance by making the untransformed commodity available to the user, and in the second by making the slightly transformed commodity available.

Since assemblage is only one step removed from brokerage it is not surprising that many of the same offices engage in both functions. In the ILAB the Foreign Service liaison officer is the one who assembles the labor packets to be sent to the labor attachés. He is also the one who assembles the ten month training program for newly selected attachés. The geographic desk officers are likewise engaged in assembly. They put together visits for foreign labor leaders, gather information requested by the Bureau of Labor Statistics or statistics needed by labor attachés. The ILAB includes a Division of International Exhibitions. This division assembles the information, personnel, and materials that go to make up an exhibit telling the story of the American labor movement to foreign audiences.

On the State Department side, the labor attachés are the chief assemblers.

These sixty FSOs on the labor beat in the foreign capitals are the primary source for gathering the raw information and data sought by the Labor Department. The attachés assemble numerical data on employment, wages, union membership, etc., for regular reports to Washington. They assemble relevant verbal information on trade union activities, industries competing with American labor, etc., for other reports. To a lesser extent the regional labor advisors in the geographic bureaus in Washington are assemblers. In passing on cables, information, and numerical data they do some sorting, aggregating, and winnowing. But to a large extent they simply pass on everything. They remain purer brokers, not attempting to add much input of their own. They are more interested in assuring the smooth flow of all information that in modifying that information.

NASA's International Affairs Office, like the ILAB, performs an assembling function. It is especially sought for its assembly of visits and trips. The State Department bombards it with a steady stream of requests to arrange visits to Houston and Cape Kennedy for foreign visitors. Since trips abroad for NASA personnel require coordination with the embassies, these are usually done as a joint project. The astronaut tours have been assembled in conjunction with the State Department's Office of Protocol and the USIA. The NASA International Office occasionally assembles training programs as it did for the United Nations members who became interested in exploiting the potential of the earth resources survey.

Trips are one of the chief commodities that the State Department assembles for NASA. While the Protocol Office handles the astronaut tours, the Science Bureau assembles the less glamorous trips. It arranged for the expedition to Mexico to study the 1970 solar eclipse. As a preliminary stage in selecting a site for a new tracking station the Science Bureau arranges visits by the NASA site survey team.

The U.N. Office assembles the delegations to international meetings on space which are sponsored by the United Nations. This includes the permanent Space Committee as well as temporary bodies. A delegation must combine the right mixture of technical expertise, diplomatic knowledge, and previous experience. This melange must be put together in the face of conflicting pressures from the various agencies demanding places. At the same time the overall size must be limited.

The State Department officials recognize assembly as part of their function. Several respondents mentioned packaging various ideas or increments of information rather than merely transmitting them in the original form. One noted that part of his job was to "put some things together." This he considered more worthwhile than simply passing them on to NASA unassembled.

The location of the assemblage function in the Treasury resembles that of the ILAB. The sixteen Treasury representatives abroad collect, sort, and pass on information and data in a fashion similar to that of the labor attachés. The main difference is that the Treasury representatives can bypass the State Department since they are not FSOs. The Treasury geographic desk officers assemble information following the same pattern displayed by the ILAB desk officers.

The State Department devotes much more effort to assembling financial information than it does to assembling labor information. Abroad each embassy includes an economic section nearly as big as its political section. The information and data assembled by these economic sections are sent home to the Economic Bureau. Duplicate information and data go to the Treasury. The sixteen Treasury representatives are intended to supplement the economic sections in countries of particular importance to international finance. They are not intended to replace the embassy's economic section for information gathering purposes.

The State Department's right to name delegations to international financial meetings is honored in the breach. The Treasury tends to unilaterally assemble its own delegations when the meetings are strictly financial, claiming that this right is within its sphere of influence. When delegates must be drawn from different departments, the Treasury and the State Department have often previously established formulas for the distribution of the positions. Each agency has a fixed number of slots assigned. The distribution among departments is not determined anew each time an individual delegation is named. Actually this is not so different from other areas. The State Department's U.N. Office has limited discretion in naming delegates to the Space Committee. Certain agencies have established expectations of a seat.

Refining

The refined commodities of Group 3 are still further removed from the basic commodities of Group 1. Accordingly their bureaucratic manufacturers are further removed from the pure brokerage function. While many of the same offices manufacture these commodities as transmitted the basic commodities, other offices and branches are being added. In the domestic departments many of these are outside the international affairs bureau.

In the Labor Department the Bureau of Labor Statistics joins the several offices noted thus far as sources of brokerage and assemblage productivity. The Bureau of Labor Statistics is very much a manufacturer of Group 3 commodities. It refines the raw data collected by the labor attachés into statistics. It refines the information gathered abroad into monographs on labor in a particular country. The Bureau of Labor Statistics is highly esteemed both within and without the Labor Department. The ILAB geographic offices consider the back-up of the Bureau of Labor Statistics to be one of their principal assets in dealing with the State Department.

To be sure, the ILAB geographic desks manufacture refined commodities of their own, principally advice and papers. They can advise on the significance of a shift in a foreign trade union's leadership, on whether American aid is trickling down to the workingman or whether the AFL-CIO sponsored AIFLD program is being well received. To justify its budget request the ILAB quantifies some of the commodities it provides for the State Department. In fiscal year 1969 the geographic desks furnished 892 "international situation responses." During the same period they supported 175 labor attachés and labor reporting officers in the embassies abroad. A similar quantification of the Office of International Organizations "included the development of 711 position papers and the support of 249 delegates to international conferences."[7]

The ILAB's support of the American delegation to the International Labor Organization took a melodramatic turn when in 1966, much to the consternation of the ILAB, the American worker delegate to the ILO walked out of the plenary session to protest the election of a Communist to the presidency. The American government delegate (the Assistant Secretary for International Labor Affairs and head of the ILAB) along with the American employer delegate remained in the meeting and tried to persuade the worker delegate to return. Meanwhile President Johnson called George Meany to the White House to ask him to end the walkout. The president told Meany that the continued walkout was undermining U.S. influence in the ILO. Finally nineteen days later, and heartened by his reelection to a three year term on the ILO Executive Committee, the wayward worker returned.[8]

In the embassies abroad it is the labor attaché who is the chief producer of advice, papers, and negotiations. Where no labor attaché is assigned a labor reporting officer assumes these duties. In Washington the labor advisor in the geographic bureau will to some extent be a manufacturer of refined commodities. But in comparison to the resources available a mile away in Federal Triangle, the State Department's geographic bureau labor advisor will seem less qualified. Hence he will produce only minimal amounts of refined commodities. For the most part he will obtain them from the Labor Department via his contact with the ILAB regional desk officer. Neither is the Labor Office a notable producer of Group 3 commodities. The Group 3 commodity the Labor Office produces is political support. Its speciality is maintaining contacts with 16th Street. The Labor Office produces trade union support by serving as a watchdog for labor interests in foreign relations. In the immediate post-war era the union and State Department interests were thoroughly intermeshed. Trade unionist Irving Brown went to France and Italy in 1945 as a labor advisor to the recovery effort. He was extensively involved in establishing anti-Communist unions. His support for the Marshall Plan extended to strike breaking in Marsailles when a communist stevedore union refused to unload American supplies.[9] Serafino Romualdi had gone to South America even earlier. An Italian immigrant himself and long time employee of the International Ladies Garment Workers staff, Romualdi went to Argentina in 1941 to rally Italian immigrants against fascism. After Pearl Harbor he served in the OSS and the State Department's Office of Inter-American Affairs.[10] The close relation between the State Department and the unions continued after the war ended. Although the State Department and the AFL-CIO have been gradually drifting apart, a number of joint projects still remain. AIFLD is one. AIFLD is the acronyn for the American Institute for Free Labor Development. Its purpose is to train labor leaders from Latin American countries. Its orientation is militantly anti-Communist. Romualdi was its first head. As originally set up AIFLD was to be supported equally by labor, business, and government. In 1967 it was exposed as one of the "CIA orphans." The CIA money was reputedly transferred to the Michigan Fund, thence to AIFLD. Since that time AID has picked up the lost funding.[11]

AIFLD came under attack by Senator William Fulbright in hearings on the foreign aid appropriations in 1969. Senator Fulbright charged that the $28 million included in the AID appropriation for support of AIFLD over the previous eight years was a "payoff" for Meany's support of the Kennedy-Johnson administration's Vietnam policy. Meany rebutted that the accusation was a "gratuitous insult to the American labor movement." "The money is used to carry out the foreign policy of the United States Government." "We believe that free trade unions are a guarantee of a free society and that free societies are in the interest of the United States, especially in the Western Hemisphere."[12] Despite the total of $33 million that has gone to support AIFLD and its two sister organizations, AALC (the African-American Labor Center) and AAFLI (the Asian-American Free Labor Institute) the tightly interlocking control of the post-war period is loosening. The State Department's Labor Office is becoming more of a broker and less able to automatically conjure up political support.

The NASA International Affairs Office is even less of a producer of refined commodities than the ILAB is. In part this is because it is smaller. It lacks the manpower to generate as much advice and as many papers as the ILAB. In part this is because of the different nature of the subject matter. Labor facts are often "soft," where space facts are "hard." An ILAB geographic desk can develop a fair amount of expertise by carefully following the events in a particular country for a while. Since each country's labor movement is unique, familiarity with the specific personalities, organizations, and events gives the desk officer an advantage in expertise resembling a monopolistic position. He knows labor affairs in country X and no one else does. Knowledge in space science is of a contrasting sort. It is not unique to the specific country but universal in its application. The mechanics of a tracking station are the same whether it be in Spain or Zanzibar. There is no set of circumstances unique to each country that it would be useful for a NASA geographic desk to master. Instead the critical knowledge is technical. Does the location give the best angle to the satellite? What are the atmospheric conditions? Is there radio interference? This technical knowledge comes from other bureaus of NASA.

The International Affairs Office does manufacture some Group 3 commodities. It organizes some routine meetings. Astronaut trips abroad have become so commonplace that the State Department no longer offers briefings except prior to major journeys. The International Office briefs the less distinguished NASA travelers.

In comparison to its NASA counterpart, the State Department's Science Bureau is a more fecund producer of refined commodities. It advises the country desks and the embassies on the impact of NASA projects affecting them. It advises NASA on State Department policy as it affects its projects. Where gaps exist in the scientific application of a policy, the Science Bureau fills them in. Like all Foggy Bottom's bureaus it is a prolific report manufacturer. For example, after the return of the ill-fated Apollo 13 the Science Bureau prepared a memorandum on the flight's effect on American foreign relations. The report noted the favorable aspects of cooperation, image, and public attention. Many nations helped by putting their navies on alert, diverting their merchant ships, and maintaining radio silence. By its skillful handling of the emergency NASA won the world's admiration for its technical abilities and discipline. The drama of the emergency dominated public consciousness. The USIA estimated that more television viewers watched the Pacific splashdown than watched the Apollo 11 moon walk nine months before. The full media coverage demonstrated the openness of American democracy.[13]

The Science Bureau is not directly involved in the assorted negotiations the State Department conducts for NASA overseas. This is conducted by the embassies. Once the embassy and the foreign government settle on the terms of the agreement, it is formalized in an exchange of notes between the ambassador and the foreign minister. The text of this agreement allowing the NASA facility will be quite specific with regards to real estate, rights to the radio spectrum, and personnel arrangements, but it will be rather vague as to the operations of the facility. That remains to be determined by NASA, in cooperation with the foreign country's science ministry if need be.[14]

State's U.N. Office and Legal Bureau back up the delegates to the Legal Subcommittee of the Space Committee through the preparation of position papers. While the Washington State Department offices produce advice and analysis, they do not conduct the negotiations. This is done by the delegation in New York, or wherever the subcommittee chooses to meet. The Legal Subcommittee chose Geneva to negotiate the Astronauts Return Agreement.

One of the State Department's biggest producers of refined commodities in the space field is the Office of Telecommunications in the Economic Bureau. The Telecommunications Office generates the advice and papers relating to Intelsat. Basically these involve legal analysis of the international law just beginning to develop in the space field. It involves interpretation of the Intelsat enabling legislation, the Interim Agreement subscribed to by Intelsat Consortium members, and many other forms of space law. The initiation of a new organization such as Intelsat is fraught with complications. The communications via satellite must be meshed with the existing system of allocation of the radio spectrum, the property rights of the transoceanic cable companies, and legal rights. The United States is constrained from agreeing to certain proposals relating to control of direct television broadcasting from a satellite because it would violate the free speech provisions of the Bill of Rights. Yet if the agreement is modified to guarantee free speech the effect will be to extend the First Amendment rights to the entire world. Some governments do not want the First Amendment intruding.

Like the Telecommunications Office, the Treasury International Office produces an impressive outpouring of advice and papers. Much of this comes from the geographic desks. Like their counterparts in the ILAB, the Treasury desks are analysts of the problems unique to each particular country. The same reason of specificity of the facts and an impressionistic style of analysis that made it possible for the ILAB desks to develop independent expertise apply here. The Treasury desks are spread thinner than the Labor desks. This makes developing a thorough understanding of one particular nation harder. While like the ILAB, the Treasury does have geographic desks, it does not put so much emphasis on them as Labor does. Instead the Treasury depends more on its offices which view the world in functional, rather than geographic, terms. It analyzes financial problems in accounting categories which cut across national and regional boundaries: the balance of payments, gold and foreign currency exchange, international economic organizations.

One of these is the Office of International Economic Activities. It focuses on trade, including PL 480. The advice it generates is both substantive and strategic. For example it prepared one paper on the impact which the DISC proposal would have on exports. It simultaneously advised on whether Congress would accept the new policy. In the PL 480 field this office prepares the Treasury position papers regarding the terms on loans to be granted to finance agricultural sales. The final U.S. bargaining position is hammered out by the ISC—the Interdepartmental Staff Committee. Legislation requires that PL 480 sale terms should move toward a full repayment in U.S. dollars instead of payment in the local currency.[15] The Treasury favors this all-dollar repayment. The Department of Agriculture generally favors less demanding terms: repayment in local currency, lower down payment, a longer repayment schedule. These make it easier to sell the surplus grain.

In the State Department the Economic Bureau is the manufacturing center for financial advice and papers. One of its main activities was drafting legislation. It wrote the parts of Nixon's trade bill pertaining to international finance and trade. The Monetary Affairs branch was particularly involved with the DISC proposal. The State Department was concerned that the trade bill, if enacted, be acceptable internationally. First the provisions had to be legal under GATT. Second it must not upset the world trade system. The provisions had to be equitable to the United States' trading partners. Within the State Department the Monetary Affairs branch manufactures advice for the geographic bureaus in technical areas beyond their competence, such as debt rescheduling, currency exchange rates, and IMF affairs.

FSOs in the Economic Bureau view these functions as manufacturing advice rather than brokerage. When asked if his office played the role of a broker, one official replied: "No, because a broker takes market forces where he finds them and tries to act as a catalyst. We try to put in some ideas of our own." Another FSO, when asked the same question, answered: "No, I am a political scientist supervising the development of economic policy." A third official, in a different office, denied he was "middleman." His job was to turn out political and economic analysis.

Innovation

The uneven distribution of producers seen in Group 3 commodities is even more pronounced with respect to the production of Group 4 commodities. The entire labor field, both in the Labor Department and the State Department, produces essentially no invented commodities. The area is in a state of regression. No new programs are being begun. Established programs are being cut back. Current ILAB effort centers in brokerage. Less effort is devoted to assembly and refining. Basically none is devoted to inventing new commodities. Although arranged by the ILAB, the regional labor attaché conferences cannot be classified as invented because by now they have become routinized. The 1967 New Delhi conference belonged in Group 4 since it was the first, but succeeding ones have simply been re-creations of it.

Space explorations has been the area most characterized by invention. The technical innovation in astrophysics has called forth matching innovations in foreign relations to meet the technical challenges. When the earth resources survey satellite program stirred world's imagination, it created demands for its immediate application. Faced with the pressure from the underdeveloped nations demanding immediate application of the ERS benefits to those particular problems, the NASA International Office organized the 1968 meeting in Vienna under the U.N. Space Committee's auspices.[16] The United Nations, in the opinion of one NASA official interviewed, contributed little beyond the prestige of its name. The International Office organized the entire conference itself. It selected the topics, solicited applicable scientific papers, screened and edited those papers submitted, and sponsored their presentation.

Much of the business of the State Department revolves around the preparation of contingency plans. As mentioned in chapter 2, the Science Bureau developed plans in the event that Apollo 13 failed to return to earth safely. The Science Bureau and the India desk set up procedures for the direct television broadcast satellite system for India. The Office of Telecommunications helped to restructure the commercial communications system in light of the introduction of Intelsat.

The position of innovation in finance is midway between that of labor and that of space. There is some production of Group 4 commodities but not as much as in the space field. In the Treasury the International Office is not particularly active in inventing commodities. For a large part this is because the Treasury has dealt with the problems in the past and has previously developed the necessary procedures. In other words the commodities have been routinized already. The Treasury International Office does not often need to organize new conferences comparable to NASA's 1968 Vienna meetings because it already has a series of international conferences. The central bank heads from the major industrial nations meet each month in Basle, Switzerland. The finance ministers of these countries likewise have their own regular fraternity sessions. In a sense these meetings are the routinization of the Bretton Woods Conference. The Treasury was so successful in inventing the 1944 conference that its offspring precluded the need to repeat the effort until the 1971 Smithsonian meeting which presided over the devaluation of the dollar. Even this called for little innovation. The International Monetary Fund established at the 1944 conference is still officially the same. The Treasury does, however, still invent some commodities. The DISC is one example. The special drawing rights are another.

The State Department's Economic Bureau is a source of invented commodities. A current proposal is to give tariff preference to imports from underdeveloped nations. The idea has come up at international meetings. The Economic Bureau is working on ways to operationalize the scheme. Among other things the goods would need a certificate of origin to prove that they were actually produced in the underdeveloped nations and not being transshipped from an industrial nation.

Bureaucratic production assumes many diverse forms. It ranges from inventions of tariff schemes such as this one for aiding underdeveloped nations to the brokerage of the ILAB Foreign Service liaison officer and from the negotiation of a treaty to the presentation of an exhibit overseas. The various bureaus tend to specialize in different forms of production. Brokerage is a particular focus of the international affairs branches of the three domestic departments. They strive to bring together the bids and offers of their own departments with those of the State Department. In every department the geographic desks are particularly active as brokers. Assemblage is favored by personnel in the embassies abroad, as well as many personnel in Washington. Refining tends to be a specialty of the core bureaus of the four departments, often outside the international affairs branches: the Bureau of Labor Statistics, NASA's Tracking and Data Acquisition Office, the Internal Revenue Service, and State's Economic Bureau and U.N. Office. Innovation is found most notably in NASA and State's Science Bureau, reflecting the developmental nature of space exploration. Yet whatever form production takes, the ultimate purpose is to enhance the value of the bureaucratic commodities produced.

Price

When Senator Fulbright accused George Meany of having been bought he named the price for the alleged payoff. Meany supposedly gave his support to the Kennedy-Johnson administration's Vietnam policy in return for $28 million. AID had transferred this amount to the AFL-CIO's AIFLD project over the previous eight years.[1] From this a cynic would note that everyone has his price; Meany's was $28 million. Observing the same exchange, an economist would note that every exchange has its price; this one's terms were easier to measure.

A price is a ratio of the commodities exchanged.[2] When, as in this case, one of the commodities is money, it is easier to measure. When neither of the commodities is money the price must be expressed in different terms. In bureaucratic exchange the latter is frequently the case. No convenient yardstick exists to measure the commodities traded. Consequently the ratio of exchange is elusive. Added to this is a second difficulty. Bureaucratic exchange is a continuing flow of commodities between the various producers rather than a series of clearly delineated *quid pro quo* trades. The balance sheet is seldom computed explicitly. The result is uncertainty as to the exact terms of the exchange. Yet while prices remain vague the bureaus do use them in evaluating their exchange. The officials questioned about specific exchanges expressed strong opinions as to whether the exchange ratio was satisfactory or not.

The Participating Agency Service Agreements (PASAs) between the Labor Department and AID furnish clear illustrations of price. Since AID is giving the Labor Department money in return for its services, there is an easily measured commodity to use as a yardstick. A PASA assigning a manpower economist to Saigon provides for a two year assignment at a price of $58,000. Another PASA provides for the Labor Department to supply a wage and income consultant to Brazil for three weeks at a price of $1,950. A third provides for a DOLITACer to be assigned to Seoul for one year to plan labor development, at a price of $25,650.[3] Each of these PASA provides for a certain ratio between the commodities exchanged: x months of service in return for y dollars.

NASA provides some commodities whose price can be expressed in dollars since they involve an exchange of a NASA produced commodity for money. When NASA launches an Intelsat rocket the international consortium repays NASA in dollars. The exchange ratio is easily measurable. The price for the launch is x dollars. NASA pays the U.S. Navy for the service it performs in recovering a returned Apollo command module. The Navy can quote the price of renting an aircraft carrier for a few days. In a similar fashion NASA can quote a price for photographing a patch of land for analysis of its crops, forests, and oil potential as part of the earth resources survey program.

The prices of other commodities NASA offers in the bureaucratic market place are more elusive because they are not exchanged for money. Astronauts are a valuable commodity. The State Department is eager to obtain their services for international tours. They are especially valuable at the present because worldwide opposition to American fighting in Indochina has blocked off alternate channels of access. But their exact price is hard to determine because it is not clear for precisely what State Department produced commodity their services are being exchanged. Their price could be reckoned in terms of tracking stations. One astronaut tour is equal to six tracking stations. A moon rock is worth one station. They may be priced among themselves. A lunar returnee is more valuable than an orbiter. One Neil Armstrong is worth two James McDivitts. They may be priced over time. An astronaut is worth more immediately after he returns than a year later. Astronauts are worth more during the Vietnam war than before or after it.

Since the Treasury's business is finance it is not surprising that the price of a commodity is often found expressed in money. But since the funds bargained over do not go to the State Department but to a foreign country or international organization, the situation is not strictly analogous to the price the Labor Department charges for a DOLITACer. The money is more of an index to the policy concessions one department is making to the other in return for its support. Sometimes, as in the NAC, the support takes the form of a vote. If the Treasury will raise the amount of a loan by x dollars, the State Department will give its vote. Or in the reverse, if the State Department will trim a request x dollars the Treasury will give its vote. Outside the NAC the configuration of the support is less neatly packaged into the form of a vote. The concession of one agency will earn more enthusiastic support from the other. A change in the level of a loan requested by one will cause the other to withdraw its objections.

In recommending that the Secretary of the Treasury cast his vote in favor of a loan, the NAC considers the price of that loan to the United States. Certain of the international banks are primarily financed by the United States; others have international backing. Hence some loans are cheaper because the money comes mostly from non-American sources. Since the World Bank has funds of its own, the price to the United States is low. Thus the NAC is more willing to approve a World Bank proposal. On the other hand since the Fund for Special Operations is chiefly supported by the United States, the price of approving one of its loans is high. Accordingly the NAC is less willing to do so.

The intensity with which a position is held is a form of price. The State Department frequently maintains a position very strongly in order to try to secure more in return from the Treasury. The Treasury will yield to a strongly held State Department "policy" position. In effect it has paid the high price demanded by the State Department.

The Determination of Price

While these foregoing examples illustrate the existence of price phenomenon in bureaucratic exchange, they do little to explain how price is determined. Price is determined by demand, yet the form that this demand takes depends on the structure of the market.

Alchian and Allen divide markets into two ideal-types in terms of the demand conditions viewed by an individual seller. These are price-taker's and price-searcher's markets.[4] In a price-taker's (or atomistic) market the producer can sell all he wants at the market price as determined by the aggregate supply and demand. In other words, he takes the market price. When this situation is drawn on a graph, the demand curve is flat.

The second type is a price-searcher's market. The seller cannot dispose of all his output at a single price. As he sells more the market price drops. His sales affect the price, driving it downward. Hence he must search for a price that will maximize his profit. When drawn on a graph the demand curve is downward sloping to the right (i.e., negative).

Alchian and Allen's dichotomy between price-takers and price-searchers is illustrated in two different instances of personnel recruitment. The Foreign Service recruits its future diplomats in a price-taker's market; AID recruits DOLITACers from the ILAB in a price-searcher's market.

The situation surrounding the recruitment of the new FSOs the State Department takes in each year may be compared to Alchian and Allen's first ideal-type: the price-taker's market. The individual applicant is faced with an essentially flat demand curve. The price is determined by the aggregate market demand. The aspiring diplomat must accept the market price. He cannot get more because if he demands too much his competitors will be chosen in his stead. This is a case of "infinite" elasticity since if the seller raises his asking price even slightly he will reduce his sales to zero.[5]

The market for entering personnel extends beyond the State Department to other government and private employers. The Foreign Service must compete with the Civil Service Commission, the Chase Manhattan Bank, the Standard Oil Company, etc. In the last decade this competition has driven up the starting salary that must be offered. Whereas ten years ago 80 percent of the new FSOs entered in the lowest class (FSO-8) now only 30 percent do so, and the percentage is expected to continue to drop.[6]

A price-searcher's market, Alchian and Allen's second ideal-type, is illustrated in Participating Agency Service Agreement between AID and the ILAB providing for a DOLITAC assignment. Here the seller is faced with a downward sloping demand curve. In each PASA the ILAB supplies a large enough fraction of the market to effect the price. As the ILAB tries to sell more DOLITACers it drives the price down. Whereas in the hiring of a new FSO the amount was small enough so that it did not effect the market, in the case of an AID-ILAB agreement the quantity is relatively much larger—large enough to have a noticeable impact. Since the entire DOLITAC corps including the reserve has a strength of only twenty to thirty members, the reassignment of one or two officials can have a significant consequence.

The negotiation of a DOLITAC agreement takes place in an oligopolistic market. The ILAB and AID do not have as many alternatives as they would in an atomistic situation, but they do have a few. The ILAB can find places for DOLITACers in Washington if AID does not want them overseas. AID can find economists and labor experts in other agencies or in the trade union movement, if the Labor Department will not supply them.

NASA finds itself in an oligopolistic market with respect to the foreign countries in which it hopes to kindle support for a joint space exploration. The development of the communications satellites is one instance of this. International cooperation on a permanent space station and shuttle is a second. NASA has few competitors in selling space performance. Potentially the U.S.S.R. is the most serious rival. It is the only one which can offer a technical level comparable to NASA. But the U.S.S.R. has been reluctant thus far to put any of its space wares on the market. Japan and China have been able to achieve a launch capability but are far behind. The European Launch Development Organization has not been able to develop a launch system. The remaining countries have depended on NASA technology and equipment. This makes NASA an oligopolist. Few countries want to buy its technology and equipment. Space exploration is costly; all but a few nations consider it a luxury. While many are willing to buy the benefits such as television reception or crop surveying, only a few are willing to pay for the more basic research programs. Furthermore, even when NASA offers to sell the benefits it can do so only if it offers them cheaply.

The United States ran into this problem when it began to organize Intelsat. Communication is inherently a two way proposition. The communicator needs someone to talk to. The transmitter needs a receiver. Satellite communication techniques are useless without a worldwide network on the ground. To get foreign partners for space communication the United States had to offer the technique and equipment at a price low enough for the foreign countries to afford. To bring the price down the United States made no attempt to charge the satellite users for the research and development expenses. NASA made a gift of the technology. It had followed the same policy domestically in 1962 with respect to the Telstar satellite. The American Telephone and Telegraph Company, which owned the Telstar, received the benefits of the prior research and development without cost. AT&T for its part, built the Telstar at no cost to NASA. When explaining the U.S. policy of not charging foreign nations for the research and development of the communications satellite and the space shuttle, a State Department respondent spoke in terms of market price: "They just could not afford to pay." "You would price the service right out of the market."

Treasury officials displayed a similar attitude when discussing terms for PL

480 repayments. "You can't put too much of a squeeze on these countries" said one, referring to a recipient of American surplus agricultural output. The terms of sale are made individually for each recipient country at the time of the sale. The American bargaining position is established jointly by the departments of Agriculture, State, and the Treasury, but, as the interviewee pointed out, these countries have limited ability to repay. Accordingly the United States settles for the best price that it can in each case.

This is price discrimination. It is a necessary (but not a sufficient) condition of monopoly.[7] To the extent to which the United States is able to successfully practice price discrimination it should be considered a monopolist rather than an oligopolist. The question is whether the price discrimination is successful. In the case of space technology the United States is a monopolist as long as the U.S.S.R. stays out of the market. There are some limited signs that the U.S.S.R. is entering it. In 1968 the U.S.S.R. announced the formation of Intersputnik, an international communications satellite system drawing its membership from within the Communist bloc. The system was a Russian response to Intelsat. It is potentially open to all nations, though no non-Communist nations have yet affiliated.[8]

The United States can maintain price discrimination because it is monopolistic although not a monopolist. It is able to be monopolistic by means of product differentiation.[9] Intelsat facilities are not compatible with the Intersputnik system. The equipment is not interchangeable. Indeed one of the tenets of the Intelsat policy is that other nations are encouraged to develop regional, scientific, and special satellites as long as they are compatible with the Intelsat technology.

When the State Department decided to give its blessing to Japan's space effort, one of the major points of contention in negotiating the cooperation agreement was that the Japanese have adequate safeguards against NASA technology leaking out to a third country. This was done because the United States could not practice price discrimination if the technology could be resold. If Japan could resell to a country, then the United States could no longer sell to country X at a higher price than Japan asked. Competition between the United States and Japan would drive the price down and might cause the United States to lose the sale completely.

Agreements not to resell are also part of the terms of a PL 480 sale. If Egypt could resell American wheat to Pakistan, then the United States could no longer quote different prices to the two countries. Price in this case is more likely to refer to the terms of payment rather than the price per bushel. The price per bushel is of little importance. More crucial is the creation of counterpart funds, the amount written off in return for a military base or the amount to be spent in development projects by the receiving government. The three departments responsible for the negotiation of PL 480 agreements often do not agree among themselves what terms should be sought. The Agriculture Department's position varies. Usually it wants easy terms so that it can sell more wheat, but sometimes it wants accelerated payment schedule so that its accounts look better for congressional scrutiny. The Treasury, concerned with the balance of payments, feels that the State Department is not tough enough. "The State Department believes that we should get a little less, never a little more," complained one bureaucratic heir of Alexander Hamilton.

The Treasury official's complaint that the State Department is soft on foreigners has an economic explanation.[10] The State Department is indeed soft on foreigners; it offers them the service of taking their side in interdepartment negotiations because it has been forced to do so by the threat from its competition. In effect the State Department is lowering its price by offering more service for the same price. This is an illustration of monopsony. In this case there is one buyer, the foreign government, and two sellers, the U.S. State Department and the foreign nation's foreign ministry. There is competition between the American embassy abroad and the foreign embassy in Washington. The American embassy tries to give better service so that the foreign government will use it in preference to using its own embassy in Washington. The two embassies are each brokers competing against each other for the patronage of the foreign government. Good service here means advocating the foreign government's complaint. By giving more service for the standard price the United States embassy is effectively lowering its price so that it can handle more of the foreign country's business. To the Treasury official the embassy has worked itself into a position of betraying American interests. The FSO views it differently. For him to advance in his career he has to earn a reputation for satisfying foreign governments. Every message the foreign government sends via him is a plus; every message sent via the foreign embassy in Washington is a minus. To the FSO it matters not whether the message is a compliment or a complaint. So long as he is getting the brokerage fee he is advancing his own career.

Money can be involved in the pricing process in two ways. The first is as a commodity itself. The ILAB receives approximately three million dollars annually in transfers from other agencies.[11] Some, for example, comes from the State Department's Cultural Bureau to compensate the ILAB for hosting labor leaders from abroad invited under the auspices of the foreign visitor program. Other funds come from AID and the Department of the Army.

The second way is as a measure of some other commodity. The value of personnel being exchanged is usually priced in terms of their salaries. Frequently the two ways are combined. The first agency gives money and the second agency gives some other commodity priced in terms of money.

Pricing a commodity in terms of money offers an easy way to make comparisons. Another easy way to compare is to exchange like commodities. Agencies often exchange a vote for a vote, a favor for favor, an invitation for an invitation, gossip for gossip. A labor member of a Foreign Service promotion board can vote to promote a consul in return for the Commerce Department representative's vote to promote a labor attaché. The Treasury answers public inquiries addressed to the State Department in return for the State Department answering questions sent to them. NASA invites Science Bureau officials to its meetings in return for that bureau's invitation to attend State Department meetings. The State Department reveals order of battle intelligence in return for comparable information from the domestic agencies.

As the commodities exchanged become more unlike the problem of pricing becomes more complex. Does a trip to New York to attend the U.N. Space Committee meeting equal a trip to Cape Kennedy to watch an Apollo launching? Does a PL 480 sale of wheat to Taiwan equal a sale of cotton to Korea?

Many bureaucratic exchanges neither involve money nor are of like commodities. These are harder to price. In general the difficulty of pricing is correlated with the degree to which the commodity is transformed. Group 1 commodities are the easiest to price; Group 4 ones are the hardest. Money, the easiest of all to price and the frequent measure of other commodities, is in Group 1. So are goods and personnel, votes and vetoes. Visits, trips, training programs, and exhibits are harder to evaluate. Image and political support are equally difficult to price. Advice is even harder because it is so specific. Contingency planning adds the uncertainty of the future to the problems of specificity. The transformation continuum furnishes only a rough guide to the ease with which a commodity may be priced. There are many exceptions. While votes and vetoes, two commodities which are the institutionalized forms of controls over the flow of other commodities, are easy to price, three other Group 1 commodities—licenses, credentials, and guarantees of professional standards—are hard to price. Papers and diplomatic negotiations are easier to set a price on than advice, image, or political support, although all are in Group 3.

The Functions of Price

The price system has two functions: (1) to clear the market and (2) to allocate resources.[12] Market clearance means that a commodity be priced so that there are just enough buyers to purchase it and just enough of the commodity to satisfy everyone willing to pay that price. The amount available should match the amount demanded. A commodity priced too high will not be completely sold. One priced too low will be gone while there are still unsatisfied buyers remaining. The Treasury, as befits the financial arm of the executive branch, is especially concerned that bureaucratic commodities should be offered at market clearing prices. This was illustrated a few years ago in a series of meetings with the State Department to determine the proper level of support for the International Development Association. Congress was to be asked to appropriate 40 percent as the U.S. contribution. Both the Treasury and the State Department thought that the time had come for a major replenishment of the IDA funds.

Both agreed that there should be balance of payments safeguards. The difference between the two departments was the amount of the appropriation. The State Department proposed "the big number." Mere mortals, unaccustomed to high finance, would express this as one billion dollars. The IDA was to get this amount each year for three years. The Treasury, on the other hand, wanted "achievable goals." It proposed "six, eight, and one." This, in the argot of the respondent, meant $600 million the first year, $800 million the second year, and one billion dollars the third year. At this point the World Bank was consulted since it had to raise matching funds from the other nations which were also contributors to the IDA account. The World Bank opted for the Treasury's "six, eight and one." It felt that it would be hard enough to raise this sum, let alone "the big number." The end result was that the World Bank was able to raise only $400 million each year. The United States' share was $160 million each year, to which Congress agreed.[13] A Treasury official questioned about this explained that the Treasury favored the largest possible appropriation for the IDA but thought that its proposal was the most that Congress would approve. The Treasury objective in these meetings was to lower State Department's proposed price to one that it knew would more easily clear the market.[14]

One market that the Treasury is responsible for clearing is that of the PL 480 counterpart funds. The Treasury acts as a collection agent for the Agriculture Department. Each buyer of surplus wheat, corn, etc., deposits its payments in the local currency. The Treasury must continually work to see that these foreign currencies are not allowed to accumulate but are used for the debts of the U.S. government. This is difficult since the PL 480 agreements usually restrict the uses to which the receipts may be put. When too much foreign currency piles up from PL 480 sales the Treasury clears the market by lowering the price. It lowers the price abruptly by declaring the currency to be in excess of the needs of the U.S. government. Ten currencies are considered excess at present. When a currency is listed as excess it is available to any department that can persuade the Office of Management and Budget and Congress to let it have some. In effect the Treasury has reduced the price from the official foreign currency exchange rate to whatever bureaucratic commodities the various departments can persuade the OMB and Congress to accept. When an appropriation of excess foreign currency is small the Treasury does not care how the funds are spent, but when an appropriation is large the Treasury is concerned that the program not be so large that it will be a drain on the resources of the foreign country. The regional labor attaché conferences discussed previously were paid for with excess foreign currency funds. In effect the rupees and dinars spent were virtually free to Labor and State. The Treasury had discounted them drastically in order to clear the market. The only costs involved were those demanded by the OMB and a reluctant House Appropriations Subcommittee before they would approve the scheme.

The excess currency situation is an unstable condition. Eager agencies will soon use up the excess leaving the Treasury supply depleted. In this case, that is the objective of the Treasury in offering the currencies at a large discount. Once the surplus is consumed the Treasury will remove that currency from the list of those in excess and conditions will return to a normal market.

Too high a price can be as bad for the market clearance function as too low a price. A commodity pegged too low, such as an excess currency, will sell out, leaving disappointed bidders who are unable to get any of the underpriced commodity. A commodity pegged too high will fail to sell out completely, leaving the seller with the unsold commodity still on his hands. One bureaucratic broker interviewed, whose job is to oversee personnel exchanges, noted that "it is not a good idea to get too good a deal." Too much salary, rank, or responsibility are counterproductive to the total program. They lead to an increased level of aspiration which cannot be met. The broker is unable to place all his personnel.

The second function of price is to allocate resources. The two functions are interrelated. Market clearance is the process of allocating resources in the short run. The market price is adjusted until all commodities offered can find buyers and all buyers can find commodities. In the short run the amount of commodities on the market is fixed, but in the long run it is variable. The long run problem of resource allocation is that of determining how much of each commodity to produce. The guide is price. If the market price of a commodity is consistently higher than normal, producers will increase the production of that commodity. If it is consistently lower, they will decrease its production. Each producer makes an independent decision guided by price. Economists refer to this as the principle of equal advantage.[15]

The upward mobile executives described by Robert Presthus in *The Organizational Society* are individuals highly sensitive to the principal of equal advantage. Presthus observes that the upward-mobiles flock to join newly created agencies. They want to get in on the ground floor. They believe that the new agency offers greater opportunities for advancement.[16] In other words, they can command a higher price. This is true; they can earn greater rewards in the new agency. The new agency must offer greater returns in order to attract resources (in this case personnel) away from the established agencies. Being more sensitive to price differences the upward mobiles come in disproportionate numbers. The price a new agency pays is not in salary alone. Government salaries are usually restrained. The new agency can offer no higher a compensation scale than the rest of the government. One way in which the new agency is able to raise its bid is to offer entry at a higher level. A GS-12 will be offered a position at a GS-14 grade. A second way is to offer a promise of greater opportunities in the future. A new agency expects to grow. Those who enter in the early period can benefit from the expansion of the agency. Since the upward-mobiles are highly attracted by power, such a new agency offers rewards additional to salary.

John Harr notes a similar preference of entering FSOs for the political specialty in accordance with the principle of equal advantage. Having the greatest rewards to offer in terms of career advancement, the political path attracts the most able entrants. Those next most able go into the general economic specialty. They avoid subspecialties such as aviation, finance, and fisheries which are considered dead ends. The administrative and consular specialties are least desirable to the upward mobile FSO.[17] Yet while entering FSOs seek the political career path, a few years later in their career the political seems less desirable because it is overcrowded. The above-normal price being offered has attracted an excessive number of personnel. At this point the more mobile FSOs seek specialties less crowded. It is at this point that some opt for the labor attaché program. Thus through a process of each FSO searching for the career specialty offering him the best price, the Foreign Service's personnel resources are distributed.

The FSO's attitude toward personnel exchanges with other agencies, as noted by Harr, similarly appears to follow the principle of equal advantage. While in general FSOs consider such work to take them outside the professional mainstream, an increasing minority have found the assignment to be a positive aid to their careers. Details outside the department gives them broader knowledge of the government, an asset in a department that nearly worships the "generalist."

The Program Planning Budgeting System is a deliberate attempt to adopt a price system for the allocation of resources within the federal bureaucracy. First introduced into the Department of Defense in 1961, the PPBS compared the prices (cost-effectiveness ratios in PPBS terminology) of various commodity packages. For example, if the objective was the defense of the Atlantic seaboard, the DOD would assemble several combinations of ships, missiles, and aircraft able to provide an equal amount of defense, then compute the cost-effectiveness fit ratio of each package. The one with the lowest cost was adopted.[18]

The problem with PPBS was that of agreeing on the prices. The DOD could make the system work because it operated in a cavalier manner. DOD systems analysts rather arbitrarily set prices for defending the Atlantic seaboard. When in 1965 President Johnson ordered the other departments to adopt the system, they were much more reluctant to declare the value of their objectives.[19] The Public Health Service, after months of discussion, finally decided that it could not set a price on a human life. The Department of the Interior was unable to declare the value of nature. The PPBS price system was not sufficient in itself to allocate resources if there were no prices established.

The Treasury, because of its particular function as the financial arm of the bureaucracy, can influence the distribution of resources from a side different from the rest of the government. Since the Treasury predicts the tax revenue the government will collect each year, it can affect the total price level of all commodities valued in money terms. The Treasury has an important say in planning all aspects of the president's budget because it knows, better than any other agency, how much money will be available. Burton Sapin suggests that the Treasury, along with the Bureau of the Budget, played a "largely negative role" in foreign affairs during the Eisenhower administration by holding down the level of foreign aid expenditures under the rationale that there would be insufficient revenue. Sapin believes that this Treasury policy reflected a conservative financial orientation of the administration.[20] When questioned about Sapin's observation Treasury respondents opined that the Treasury's conservative orientation was more a result of its financial role than the particular policy of the Eisenhower administration. One complained that "the State Department is always spawning ideas for spending money, then trying to sell them to us." Another noted that he was not really concerned with the State Department's spending; it was the DOD that worried him. A third believed that Sapin was generally right. The Treasury did influence spending decisions because of its forecasts of revenue, but its role was really fairly modest. The Budget Bureau was much more of an influence. State Department officials interviewed were more prone to see the Treasury as niggardly. They believed the Treasury was overly conservative. One expressed the opinion that the Treasury acted as if all the money spent by the entire federal government were its very own.

In the economic market place certain entrepreneurs specialize in allocating resources according to the principle of equal advantage. In this they are guided by price. Rather than wait for the original seller of a commodity to shift it from a less profitable place to a more profitable one these entrepreneurs buy the commodity in the first location and sell it in the second, thereby earning the profit themselves. This process of transferring is called arbitrage; its practitioners are arbitrageurs. The market benefits because price discrepancies are eliminated. Resources are shifted to the location where they command the best price. Arbitrage is illustrated by the world wheat market. When the price of wheat rises in Liverpool to the point where it is greater than the price in Chicago plus shipping costs, an arbitrageur will buy the wheat in Chicago and ship it to Liverpool. As more and more wheat is shipped to Liverpool the price there will fall to the point where the arbitrageur can no longer make a profit. The free market existing in foreign currencies prior to World War I was kept in adjustment through arbitrage. When the British pound brought a higher price in dollars in New York than in London, an arbitrageur would ship his pounds from London to buy dollars in New York. The present international monetary system's fixed exchange rates and currency restrictions keep private arbitrage restricted to a narrow band of 2½ percent on each side of parity. When the fluctuations excede this the government intervenes.[21]

Within the foreign affairs arena arbitrageurs shift commodities from place to place in response to the various prices being offered. The commodity of personnel is especially suitable for arbitrage. The ILAB's Program Office moves DOLITACers from one post to the next according to where they are most in demand. It brings in other Labor Department personnel temporarily for the DOLITAC reserve when demand is high and releases them when it is low. The ILAB's Foreign Service liaison office and the State-AID Labor Office serve as arbitrageurs of labor attachés. Although the assignment procedure is officially shared between the two departments, State's Labor Office tends to specialize in the more important attaché posts. In the early days of the program many labor attachés were recruited from the labor movement. Of those labor attachés abroad in the late 1950s half had been, or still were, trade union members. Of these 72 percent had held full-time staff positions in their union; 22 percent had held office in their local and 8 percent had held national office. Twenty-four percent had had preappointment careers entirely or primarily in the labor movement.[22] The bureaucratic arbitrageurs had been able to convince these men that diplomacy offered more rewards than staying with their unions. By the late 1950s the trade union's domination was beginning to wane. Since then the unionists have given way to increasing numbers of FSOs who have entered the program as a career specialty. The arbitrageurs of the ILAB and the Labor Office can no longer make the same profits because the price being offered for a labor attaché has fallen.

Planning an astronaut tour may be viewed as an exercise in arbitrage. The USIA in particular seeks to move the astronauts to the locations where they will yield the highest return. The Apollo 11 crew skimmed off the prime sites of Paris, Rome, Bombay, and Tokyo. The planners of the Apollo 12 tour therefore chose the best alternative sites remaining. The tour planners were moving their commodity from the major capitals, where the price offered was low, to other capitals, where the price was higher. Thus the Apollo 12 crew went to Lisbon, Helsinki, Rangoon, and Osaka. Within each stop the USIA sought to move the astronauts into the activities where their time would yield the highest return. The USIA sought to schedule press conferences and television shows in preference to the small ceremonial meetings favored by the State Department Office of Protocol.

Speculation may be understood as arbitrage through time. Whereas the arbitrageur allocates resources from one location to another, the speculator allocates resources from one time to another. The market benefits because a price discrepancies through time are smoothed out. Of course since the future is always to some degree unpredictable, speculation is less certain than arbitrage. Speculation is illustrated in the wheat market. The price is lowest just after the harvest and highest just before it. A speculator will buy the cheap wheat at harvest time and store it. He sells it months later when the price has risen. A broker can also speculate in foreign currencies. This is more uncertain because there is no predictable cycle of harvests and storage as in the case of wheat.[23] Presthus's upward-mobiles act as speculators when they flock to join a newly created agency. They are gambling that the development of the agency will offer them greater opportunities than they had previously. The trade unionists who became labor attachés in the post-war period and the FSOs who join the program now are speculators. They are betting that some time in the future they will enjoy greater rewards for having entered labor diplomacy. These men, however, are speculating with their own careers only. They are not quite equivalent to the arbitrageurs discussed previously who made aspecialty of allocating the resources of others.

Training programs are a means of speculation. When the ILAB presents its one allotted day of orientation on the Labor Department to newly sworn in FSOs, it is speculating. It is gambling that the effort it spends in briefing the novice diplomats will be returned in increased labor awareness when the young men go off to their first foreign duty station.

The Treasury and the State Department's Economic Bureau are speculating with the DISC proposal. They are wagering that the time and effort they devote to developing the program in papers, meetings, and international negotiations will pay off in securing approval for the scheme, first from Congress and then from GATT.

The State Department's African Bureau is speculating by encouraging NASA's limited contacts with the Union of South Africa. It is betting that the criticism the United States receives at the United Nations and at the embassies in black African countries for maintaining a NASA tracking station in the Republic will be outweighed by the access this station may provide at some time in the future.

9   Investment and Insurance

The agencies discussed in the preceding pages forego current consumption in order to have greater resources in the future. In doing this they are investing. Their goal is to increase their total wealth by shifting resources from the present to the future.[1] Upward mobile bureaucrats move to newly organized agencies in order to benefit from the expansion of these agencies. The ILAB devotes time to familiarizing novice FSOs with labor affairs so that these young diplomats will be more "labor conscious" in their foreign assignments. The State Department's Economic Bureau prepares papers and testimony in support of the DISC in order, first, to win approval for the program from Congress and GATT and, eventually, to give a tax advantage to American exporters, thereby improving the balance of payment situation. Its African Bureau encourages NASA's contacts with the Union of South Africa so that this link can be expanded into relations that will lead the Union to a more acceptable position regarding apartheid. In each of these four cases the agency invests with the objective of increasing its total resources.

Insurance may be contrasted with investment. Whereas the goal of investment is to shift resources over time to maximize future wealth, the goal of insurance is to shift resources over time to maximize future utility. A homeowner purchasing fire insurance pays for the premium with dollars having a low utility since his home and other wealth are intact. But should his home burn down he will receive dollars which have a high utility since he is homeless.[2] Adamson Hoebel describes similar systems in the Eskimo culture.[3] A successful hunter shares his prize with his less successful neighbors. Since he has so much, the meat he gives away is of low utility, but in the future he may return empty handed while his neighbor is successful. The second hunter then repays the first in meat which has high utility, for the first then has nothing. Insurance is worthwhile to the insured even though he may have contributed more dollars or meat than he ever received in return, so long as the utility of the payoff remains sufficiently high.

The goal of insurance is to counteract unpredictable, adverse events in the future. It is a way of smoothing out the chance fluxuations in the environment. This contrasts with the assumptions on which investment is predicated which are that the future is essentially foreseeable. This, of course, does not preclude one from acting on the basis of both views of the future. This mixed strategy would call for one to both invest and insure.

The dichotomy between investment and insurance follows in a general way the dichotomy between a predictable and an unpredictable future. An individual or an agency which perceives the future as predictable will be concerned with investment. New agencies appear sure to grow, therefore upward mobiles invest their careers. New labor attachés are expected to serve ten to twenty years, therefore the ILAB invests in an extensive training program. A tracking station can be counted on to track and communicate with satellites, therefore NASA invests in its construction.

As predictability gives way to unpredictability, investment gives way to insurance. Whereas investment is oriented toward the future state of the asset, insurance is oriented toward the future state of the insurer. This is another way of comparing a wealth standard to a utility standard. The insured seeks protection in the event of an unfavorable contingency. For a home owner this may be fire. For the agency this may be a disastrous budget cut. For a nation this may be the threat of war. In the light of such contingencies it is rational for an economic actor to transfer resources into holdings that are good insurance even though they are not good investments.

In some ways the concept of insurance is more useful than the concept of investment in analyzing the behavior of agencies in bureaucratic exchange. When agencies engage in shifting commodities over time their goal for the future is often greater utility rather than greater total wealth.

One reason for this orientation toward insurance rather than investment may be that agencies are not always too successful in enhancing their total wealth through investing. Agencies frequently find that their investments have been unsuccessful causing total resources to go down rather than up. Bureaucratic commodities seem to be notoriously prone to depreciate; the credit one agency has built up with another suddenly decreases when the first tries to draw against it at a later time. Millions of dollars of foreign aid proved to be worth little when in November 1971 the United States called upon the recipients to vote for its two-China proposal in the United Nations General Assembly. Robert L. Peabody similarly notes the depreciation of legislative commodities in his study of the 1965 Republican leadership change in the House of Representatives.[4] Minority Leader Halleck could not effectively cash in his credit for favors built up over the previous sessions. Halleck's investment had depreciated below the point where it would give him the majority he needed to retain his job.

Investment

Personnel is a commodity favored for investment purposes. This is manifested in recruitment, assignments, exchanges, career systems, and training. Recruitment for the combined Foreign Service is the most complex of any branch of the federal government other than the military. Entering FSOs are considered to be an important investment; the time and effort devoted to recruiting them is felt to be well spent. Despite the Labor Department's representation on the Foreign

Service selection boards, there is no indication that the process enables it to bring in future diplomats predisposed to the labor point of view. Indeed one ILAB official involved with the process expressed the opinion that most entering FSOs were hostile toward organized labor and very few were favorable. The Labor Department must defer to the broader Foreign Service standards until it reaches the stage of selecting men for its own program. In choosing labor attachés the ILAB hopes to find men with whom it will be able to work on a long term basis. The bureau looks forward to a ten to twenty year association. In the more rough and ready days of European recovery the Labor Department did not have such a long time frame. It was interested in recruiting attachés experienced in labor affairs who could go right to work fighting the Communists and promoting the Marshall Plan.

Writing in *The Forest Ranger*, Herbert Kaufman notes that the Forest Service places a high value on recruiting "men who fit." One of the concerns of the Forest Service is that the rangers conform to the service's policies. To assure this it selects a Forest Service type.[5] In the same way the State Department selects a Foreign Service type and the Labor Department selects a labor attaché type. Each agency recruits its own type to maximize the likelihood of conformity. Its own type is the best investment.

Those involved in assigning labor attachés to their posts seek to invest their joint resources most efficiently. The AFL-CIO is interested in the key posts and in the senior attachés. On one hand this is because of its concern that the United States be effectively represented in labor affairs in the most important capitals. On the other hand the AFL-CIO is interested in advancing the careers of some of its own men who are in the program. Phil Delaney of the Labor Office was for many years the attachés' guardian angel in Foggy Bottom.[6]

Many interagency personnel exchanges are an investment. The participants are sent for the purpose of broadening their experiences, often in preparation for greater responsibility. This, at least, is the rationale. In fact consequences of the exchange range from this ideal to a possible dead end for the official or the loss of a man for his agency. The NASA-State exchange comes the closest to meeting the desired objectives. The participants have been given responsible jobs in the host agency and returned to the parent agency at the end of their tour. The FSOs sent to the ILAB did not fare as well. Labor Department officials implied that they were sent chiefly because the State Department had nothing better to do with them. They were assigned only for short periods and could not become well integrated into the ILAB program in that time. The State Department exchange with the Treasury was a bad investment for Foggy Bottom. The Treasury liked the exchanged personnel so well that it invited them to stay, which they did.

The State Department approaches personnel exchanges with a different attitude than the domestic agencies. It is more eager to loan its personnel. The domestic agencies give few or none in return. The domestic agencies usually feel that they are only furnishing a place for the Foreign Service to store its officers temporarily in Washington. They often feel that this babysitting function is an inconvenience. In contrast to this general view of FSOs as a burden, the domestic agencies occasionally find their guests quite welcome. In one case the ILAB sent an FSO to North Philadelphia where he observed the anti-poverty program at first hand. At the end of his sojourn he wrote up his experiences. The ILAB found the report valuable both as an analysis of the program and as a paper useful in explaining the American anti-poverty program to labor attachés and other FSOs in the embassies abroad. With this in mind it was sent out in the labor packet.[7]

A well-structured career system is a good investment. The establishment of the Foreign Service by the 1924 Rogers Act offered a prospective diplomat a more attractive set of commodities to induce him to represent his country abroad. He was offered an organized career in place of the vicissitudes of patronage that had previously been his lot. The Rogers Act offered him the prestige of a commission, the incentive of merit promotion, and the security of a retirement pension.[8] The present status of the DOLITAC is that of a nascent career system. It began as occasional interagency contracts with AID to provide the services of labor advisors. In 1965 it was organized into the present DOLITAC—the Department of Labor International Technical Assistance Corps. In the future DOLITAC might develop into a larger, more structured corps having its own promotion system, training, and identity. If it is to do so it will be following the evolution of the Public Health Service which began in the early nineteenth century as a system of contract physicians.[9] Clearly DOLITAC has a long way to go. At present it has only eighteen regular members, exclusive of the reserve. A more likely scenario, if indeed it is to survive, would be for it to merge with the Foreign Service.

Personnel training is probably the major investment made by the four agencies under discussion. The State Department places greater emphasis on formal post-entry training than the Treasury or NASA. Much of the training is conducted by the Foreign Service Institute. The FSI offers programs in languages, area studies, foreign policy, and international relations. The Macomber task force recommends an expanded role for the FSI, including more frequent refresher courses for FSOs, seminars for senior officers, and more gaming and simulation facilities.[10]

While the State Department operates an elaborate system of formal training, little of it involves exchange with the three domestic agencies under consideration. The only significant interagency training program is that of the new labor attachés. In terms of the ratio between the investment and the return this program pays a handsome profit to the ILAB.[11] In return for ten months of training the Labor Department gets the attachés' services for the following ten to twenty years. Even if the labor attaché leaves the labor specialty to move to other areas of diplomacy, he continues to have a sensitivity to the labor point of view.

A second nest egg of agency investment is bureaucratic capital. Following the more general definition, bureaucratic capital represents produced commodities that can be used as factor inputs for further production.[12] Tracking stations are bureaucratic capital for the space agency. They are produced by the joint efforts of NASA and the State Department. Once operational they contribute to NASA's production of its other output of scientific information, communication channels, favorable image of the United States, and other commodities. According to an agency scientist interviewed, the extensive tracking network gives the United States space program two distinct benefits: First is safety in manned flights. A manned space vehicle is in continual voice contact with the ground. Second is the capability to "nurse along sick satellites." If a malfunction renders a satellite incapable of following its pre-recorded program, NASA can broadcast "actual time" commands to the satellite from whichever tracking station is then in communication with it. This alternative has been used several times after malfunctions in the Mariner and Surveyor series. This capability, according to the respondent, gives the United States a great advantage over the Russians. Because the Russians lack a round-the-world tracking station network they can only contact their satellite once a day. After transmitting the commands, they "put it to bed" until the next day. If failure occurs or the satellite needs an actual time command while communication is blocked out, there is nothing that they can do. NASA believes that the U.S.S.R. has lost a number of salvageable satellites for this reason. The U.S.S.R. can obtain 360 degree coverage by stationing a ship in a Cuban harbor or at sea in an unwatched quadrant. With the commissioning of the 45,000 ton *Cosmonaut Yuri Gagarin* in December 1971, the Soviet Union greatly expanded its tracking capabilities. The 760 foot research ship, equipped with four large dish antennas and special stabilizers for rough weather, is claimed by the Russians to be the equal of a land based tracking station.[13]

Like tracking stations, the earth resources survey program represents an investment in bureaucratic capital. The satellite and the photographic interpretation techniques have been developed by NASA. The ERS program will apply this capital to produce information about crops, forests and minerals useful to the participant nations. Intelsat is a similar program that has already reached the stage of mature productivity. NASA, with the assistance of AT&T, developed and produced the equipment. The members of the Intelsat Consortium are now utilizing the communications "hardware" to enhance their respective economies' productivity by the improved communication afforded. The direct television broadcasting to India will make use of the ATS-F satellite to produce a higher level of education among the adult population of the sub-continent.

In each of these three cases NASA invested its bureaucratic resources in producing a capital good. The profitability of the investment for the agency is difficult to measure since there is no convenient yardstick for the value of the product. In the aggregate NASA's investments in the late 1960s and early 1970s must be rated as poor in terms of the widespread budget cuts suffered by the agency since fiscal year 1965. This view, however, tells little about any particular project. Since the international programs form such a small part of the total NASA effort, the success of investment in ERS, direct broadcasting, and Intelsat defies measurement in this fashion. Indeed it may be that these three are the most profitable investments since they have found, or are in the process of finding, financial support from abroad. Intelsat, the only one sufficiently advanced to operate in a practical fashion, is now well on its way to becoming a commercial success. Present indications are that demand for the ERS and direct broadcasting are nearly as high.

In the financial field the DISC is representative of a bureaucratic investment. If approved by Congress and by GATT, the DISC will be a capital good produced by the Treasury and the State Department that will then be capable of producing a balance of payment surplus by aiding American exporters. The Treasury and the State Department will benefit by the surplus which will ease pressure on them from foreign banks and treasuries. This sort of a return on the Treasury and State Department's investment is highly roundabout, but given the complex nature of their goal, not unnecessarily roundabout.

In a sense a Treasury policy decision to manipulate the national fiscal situation is an investment. The amount of resources devoted to such a decision are small in comparison to those devoted to DISC and especially in comparison to the effects of the policy. Like many investments in the economic market, the risk is high. A small investment can lead either to large profits or disastrous losses. For example a change in the interest rate for Treasury bills can have sudden, extreme, and unpredictable consequences for the balance of payments. In a 1966 article in the *American Economic Review*, Franco Modigliani and Richard Sutch analyze the Treasury policy known as Operation Twist. The twist was a high rate for short term funds coupled artificially with a low rate for long term funds. The policy was undertaken by the Kennedy administration in 1961 to help in poor balance of payments situation. The authors conclude that the results were insignificant. The contemporaneous introduction of time certificates of deposit had a greater, albeit unintended, effect on the term structure of interest rates.[14] By 1963 the Treasury was abandoning Operation Twist. In July President Kennedy called on Congress to enact a supposedly temporary interest equalization tax. The IET was to succeed the twist as the next in a long line of weapons with which the Treasury tried ineffectually to hold back the balance of payments pressure during the 1960s.[15]

One dimension along which an investment's risk varies runs from generality to specificity. Investments with a general impact are often of high risk; those with a specific impact are usually of low risk. A Treasury change in the interest rate for Treasury bills has a general impact which is hard to predict. The negotiation of a bilateral treaty on double taxation has a specific impact which is easy to predict. Direct broadcasting to home television receivers from satellites (the next stage after the ATS-F program) will have a general impact. Hence the risk is high. It might set off a propaganda war or threaten the cultural integrity of a country.[16] Building a new tracking station has a specific impact. Risk is low. A tracking station poses little threat to the host country since all it can do is to perform its limited technical function.

Economists consider the rate of return on an investment to measure two factors. One is risk. Investors demand a higher interest rate on riskier investments.[17] To a certain extent the Treasury manipulation of fiscal policy or the DISC satisfy this test. Each has a low cost in terms of the resources devoted to its production. A shift in fiscal policy is risky because of unintended consequences. The DISC is risky because securing approval promises to be difficult. It has been before Congress twice, most recently in the 1970 Trade Bill which died in the Senate when the 91st Congress adjourned. Once Congress approves, it still faces the risk of GATT's disapproval. Yet if either of these two financial schemes does have the intended result, the payoff in terms of the American balance of payment deficit will pay a generous return on the comparatively modest resources invested.

The second factor reflected in the interest rate is the inconvenience to the investor of being temporarily deprived of the use of his resources. Even an absolutely safe investment must pay some interest to induce investors to part with their resources.[18] The Treasury will only send Internal Revenue Service personnel to negotiate a tax treaty if it believes that over the succeeding years such a treaty will repay the costs of diverting these personnel from alternate uses of their time. The Treasury feels the costs of searching out tax havens to be too high to make the effort worthwhile. Hence it depends on the State Department economic officers to uncover any havens. The Treasury sends the IRS only when the State Department has found a country in which it is worth investing its time.

Control of bureaucratic territory is often a good investment for an agency to make. Prior discussion has noted the advantages to an agency which can exercise a monopoly over a certain area. The State Department seeks to control foreign affairs; the Treasury, finance; etc. The agency exercising jurisdiction receives the benefits, is entitled to license other agencies wishing to operate in its territory, etc. When new territories open up, it offers a potential asset in which to invest.

In the mid-1960s the State Department successfully invested in developing and acquiring such a new piece of bureaucratic real estate. NASA's development of the Early Bird and other communications satellites in the early 1960s alerted the State Department to the potential of space communication.[19] The Federal Communications Commission recognized the area at the same time. The State Department gained ascendancy through representing its views as identical to those of the European partners in the space communications network. It bought off its chief rival, the FCC, by promising it the right to veto specific satellite projects. Once in control the State Department entrenched itself. Executive Order 11191 of January 4, 1965 made it the official coordinating agency for the foreign affairs aspects of the communications satellites. This effectively restricted entry into the field.

Insurance

One devotes resources to insurance to gain protection in the event of an unfavorable contingency. Just as a homeowner joins a mutual fire insurance association, so an agency forms alliances with other agencies to share the risks of a bureaucratic disaster. NASA is currently experiencing such a disaster. Its budgets have been cut each year since fiscal year 1965 and the outlook for the future continues to be bleak. Accordingly the space agency is desperately groping for help. Alliances with foreign nations seem to offer a good form of insurance. International agreements, once entered into, serve as a guarantee against budget cuts. The rigidity of the terms of international cooperation preclude Congress from trimming funds.[20] In recent years NASA has increasingly emphasized the practical applications of space technology. The earth resources survey will enable the underdeveloped nations to exploit their natural resources. The Nimbus satellite will enable all nations to enjoy accurate weather forecasting. The direct television broadcasting will bring information about modern agricultural methods, hygiene, and birth control to the people of India. NASA has combined international cooperation with the ecology movement in the international biological program. Using NASA's remote sensing equipment, the IBP will analyze the evolution of ecological systems in northern Argentina. In these applications and in the less practical ones such as the space shuttle and the Helios probe, NASA seeks to diversify its sources of support, thereby lessening the damage done by congressional budget cuts. International cooperation helps both by decreasing NASA's dependence in cases where funds come from foreign countries and by rigidifying the budget by international agreements to commit funds at a certain level.

The State Department displays a similar pattern of seeking alliances as a form of insurance. The State Department has used the labor attaché program and support for AIFLD to forge an alliance with the AFL-CIO. By maintaining a network of labor attachés in the embassies abroad and by allowing AFL-CIO to participate in the management of the program, the department has cultivated the support of organized labor. It has enhanced that support through AID's funding of approximately 90 percent of the budgets for AIFLD, AALC, and AAFLI.[21] At the same time the State Department has managed to use the labor attachés as a buffer for its core personnel by keeping the attachés in the lower status reserve category. The labor attaché's reserve commissions have made them more vulnerable to cutbacks than the regular FSOs in the political and economic specialties. Thus in periods of personnel reductions the labor attachés bear the brunt while the regular officers are protected.

The State Department has not chosen to form such strong alliances with either NASA or the Treasury. In recent years the space agency has had little to offer as an insurer, having been in a vulnerable position itself. The State Department has been able to obtain its commodities from NASA without having to commit itself to a long term alliance. The Treasury, while in a strong position, has done little to encourage the State Department to enter an alliance. It is not eager to insure Foggy Bottom. Certain State Department policies may be interpreted as commodities exchanged for Department of Defense insurance. State was for many years a strong supporter of the war in Vietnam. Dean Rusk often seemed to be a stronger advocate of the war than Robert McNamara. State has been a champion of NATO. It has led support for the policy of maintaining American units in Europe. It has sought military offset agreements to pay for the troops in the face of Treasury opposition to this drain on American reserves. This behavior suggests that the State Department considers the Defense Department to be a more desirable ally than the Treasury. Given DOD's size and growth it would be hard to challenge the State Department's choice.[22]

 **Conclusion**

An Evaluation of Microeconomic Approaches

This book began with the objective of exploring the extent to which microeconomic theories of exchange could be used to understand the process of foreign policy formulation by the federal bureaucracy. It is now appropriate to render a verdict as to how well the exchange theories have fulfilled that goal.

Microeconomics offers the political scientist an extensive set of theories which may be fruitfully applied to interaction within the bureaucracy. Utility is one of these. It gives the key to exchange—i.e., the two parties place differing values on a commodity because of their differing utility functions. A more sophisticated approach to utility using indifference curves can be specifically applied to analytically reconstruct the decision-making process in selecting a site to hold a conference or to locate a facility.

Adam Smith's famous dictum that specialization is a function of the extent of the market has applications in the foreign affairs arena. Much of the behavior of the bureaucracy involved in foreign affairs in recent years is a result of the vast expansion of the arena since World War II. This enlargement of the international sector created room for new specialties to develop. Labor was one of these. Finance, which had first emerged prior to the war, came fully of age as a specialty of the Bretton Woods conference in 1944. Space came into its own as an aspect of foreign policy after the technology was developed in the late 1950s and 1960s.

The jurisdictions of the four agencies studied—State, Labor, NASA, and Treasury—follow a pattern analogous to that of firms in a situation of monopolistic competition. Like these firms, the agencies develop product differentiation as a device for enhancing their monopoly position. They also follow the principle of differentiation by offering services that are similar but not identical to those of other agencies.

The Edgeworth box serves as a model of the interagency bargaining process. When the two parties are in a sub-optimal position (i.e., not on the contract curve) they bargain according to the rules of consensus. This sub-optimal model matches bargaining between the Labor Department and AID over the terms of the PASAs. But once the parties reach the Paretian optimum (the contract curve) the milieu changes. Bargaining becomes a conflict situation. Common interests have been exhausted. The gains of one are the losses of the other.

Viewing bureaucratic activity in terms of production serves to structure the process. Since this book has examined interagency relations, production has often taken the form of brokerage. Furthermore, international programs exhibit a tendency toward brokerage. This is hardly surprising since the activities of agencies in the foreign affairs arena are inherently projections of interaction among nations. The international affairs branches of the three domestic departments tend to emphasize brokerage more than the other bureaus within these three departments. Those core bureaus are more prone to stress assemblage and refining as their form of production. In keeping with the technical character of the entire agency, production in NASA's international affairs branch frequently takes the form of innovation.

The concept of price has been less useful than production in helping to understand the bureaucratic process. The chief difficulty centers on the lack of a common measure by which to compare the various commodities traded. While an economist has money to use as a measure, a political scientist has no such versatile yardstick by which he can evaluate the exchange ratios. Despite this disadvantage, price theory aids in understanding the allocation of bureaucratic resources. In the short run, bureaucratic arbitrageurs shift commodities from one agency to another in order to maximize the return. In the long run speculators shift commodities from one agency to another over time.

Agencies shift commodities over time in order to successfully invest. They seek to maximize their total wealth. But in the cases considered in this study investment has not been a particularly successful activity. Bureaus which engage in it have often found their total resources diminished rather than enhanced. In contrast bureaus have often been more successful in insuring. Because international programs involve long term commitments of support, the three domestic departments under study frequently have favored such programs. They seek the rigidity entailed as a guarantee against budget cuts. NASA, because of its generally declining budget, has been increasingly eager to undertake joint programs abroad.

This brief summary reviews some of the ways in which microeconomic theories of exchange can be used to understand the foreign policy formulation process. But many other aspects remain for future research.

Topics for Future Research

Thorstein Veblen was the first to systematically consider the issue of display. Since he published *The Theory of the Leisure Class* in 1899 many other economists have pondered the problem.[1] Some refer to display as an irrational aspect of exchange, but, rational or not, it seems to be an inherent aspect. Display serves several purposes applicable to bureaucratic, as well as economic, activity. First is as an aid to valuation. The hearings before the congressional appropriation committees are of this sort. The agencies go up to Capitol Hill to display their programs publicly so that the committees may determine the price the agency is worth for the coming year. In a similar fashion NASA's International Affairs Office and the State Department translate the technical requirements for a tracking station into terms of its impact on the host country's economy. The American embassy displays the proposal for the NASA facility so that the host government may evaluate it. On occasion failure to display may imply that a commodity has a high value. Secrecy may increase its apparent value. One official interviewed commented that one of his current problems was "how to sneak something into print." The clandestine commodity alluded to was a bit of possibly controversial information which might cause the United States embarrassment if it were discovered to be a secret but would be considered trivial if it could be quietly slipped into an already wordy congressional hearing or into an obscure technical journal. Casual display would lower the price of the commodity and thereby defuse the potential controversy.

Display's second function is as an incentive to enter into the exchange. Merchants display their merchandise on counters or advertise it on television. The State Department displays its product—the United States—by sending astronauts on world tours, showing a lunar sample at Expo 70, and posting labor attachés overseas. The ILAB has a Division of International Exhibitions to arrange its displays. Foreign labor leaders are invited to visit the United States to see the labor movement at first hand. Taking its cue from the image conscious FBI, the State Department encouraged a television series featuring George Hamilton as a dedicated, glamorous young FSO. Presumably these various forms of display overseas encourage foreign nations to contribute money for space exploration, cooperate with the AFL-CIO, aid the weak American dollar, and at home similarly encourage the television watching public to urge their congressmen to vote more funds for the FSO corps.

The third function of display is as a substitute for a commodity.[2] At the Chicago Board of Trade thousands of bushels of wheat will change owners without either party actually seeing the grain. The exchange will be effected through the display of the wheat in the form of warehouse receipts. The receipt proves the existence of the commodity. In a similar fashion a labor attaché in a foreign capital "proves" that the State Department is representing the interests of American labor; the Labor Department's seat on the Board of Foreign Service "proves" that labor has a voice in the management of the foreign service. The creation of the post of Deputy Assistant Secretary of Labor for Trade and Adjustment policy "proves" the Nixon administration's interest in workers threatened by foreign competition. It is not enough for the administration to say that it is concerned; it had to give a visible sign. The sign was a reshuffling of the boxes on the Labor Department organization chart.

Finally display may be used as a commodity itself. It is frequently used to confer status. The diplomatic corps has traditionally placed a high value on the symbols of status. An ambassador is called "your excellency" and rides in a limousine with flags on the fenders. The labor attaché, having less status, gets a diplomatic passport and a "Corps Diplomatique" plaque on his automobile.

Game theory is another area for future research. It has often been advanced as a fruitful approach to the study of decision making by economic actors.[3] Presumably the numerical basis of economics should lend itself conveniently to the application of game theory. The choices open to a firm in the market may be likened to the choices open to the player of a game. Depending on the state of the market, the position may be analogized to two-person or n-person games, zero-sum or non-zero-sum games, cooperative or conflict games. The decision maker may be faced with certainty or uncertainty. He may act alone or as a member of a group. The chief difficulty with applying game theory to bureaucratic behavior via microeconomics is that the economists have not found many applications themselves. The weakness of game theory is in its inability to cope with n-person, non-zero-sum games under conditions of uncertainty. Since it is just this sort of situation that makes up so much of the world faced by the economic actor, it is understandable that the economists have been so little able to apply game theories. Hence economists have little to offer political scientists in this area.

Game theory, however, does offer some useful insights into decision making in the firm that has applications to decision making in the bureaucracy. Risk is one of these. As mentioned in chapter 3 a risk orientation is sometimes a better explanation of a decision than a utility. A matrix of risk payoffs may look considerably different than a matrix of utility payoffs. The penalty for failure may far exceed the reward for success.[4] Of the four departments under consideration, the State Department seems to be the most guided by a risk orientation. At least in part this may be attributed to its role of receiving the complaints in cases of failure. When a policy produces foreign backlash the State Department is the first to feel the sting.

The problem of public goods has been attracting attention recently. A public good is a commodity produced collectively whose benefits are available to all (i.e., none can be excluded). Mancur Olson has developed a theory of collective action based on the premise that as the size of a group increases it increasingly suffers from the free rider problem.[5] This means that a member of the group can enjoy the benefits even if he ceases to contribute. The foreign affairs arena is particularly afflicted with the free rider problem. The basic goals of foreign policy—peace, access, security, etc.—are intrinsically collective commodities. The more specific policy objectives of the international programs of the three domestic departments studied also tend to be public goods. New knowledge of space cannot, at least under the present NASA policy of openness, be denied to members of the world scientific community regardless of whether they contributed to the American space program. The benefits of a stable international monetary system cannot be withheld from a single nation that refuses to cooperate.

Frohlich and Oppenheimer have criticized Olson's conception of the free rider problem.[6] They conclude that the key to the supply of public goods is the expectation of the member as to the amount the other members will contribute. If a group possesses a mechanism which will guarantee the contributions of the others, the individual member will continue to contribute regardless of the size of the group. Frohlich and Oppenheimer foresee "the emergence of a political entrepreneur whose profits are tied to the supply of such goods." These entrepreneurs would presumably be the equivalent of the brokers discussed in chapter 8. The application of the public goods insights might help to explain brokerage in the cases of larger groups. For example, the NAC secretary serves as a broker among twelve or more agencies operating in the finance sub-arena. This size may already be a large enough group to produce the problem of free riders. The application of theories of collective choice may thus be appropriate.

Olson suggests that one way in which groups cope with the free rider problem is by developing by-products which are sufficiently attractive to the members to assure their continued support.[7] In a 1966 article he and Richard Zeekhauser proposed that NATO seek to increase its non-collective by-product as a means of encouraging certain members to contribute more.[8] In other cases the by-product may not necessarily be viewed as an asset by all members. As discussed in chapter 7 the State Department's insistence that the Intelsat Consortium articles of agreement guarantee rights of free speech in its communication satellites is viewed by some consortium members as an undesired extension of the U.S. Constitution's First Amendment.

Another area for future research is the question of how policy formulation by means of exchange fits in with other sorts of decision making. One view of this may be obtained by drawing a continuum from one-time decision making on the right to flow decision making on the left (see figure 10-1). The axis thus runs from the case of one big decision made at a single point in time to a series of smaller decisions made over a long period of time. Constitution writing is an example of the former. A constitution is a major agreement covering a multitude of issues made at a single time designed to govern for a long period thereafter. The men participating in the writing are self-consciously aware of their roles as "founding fathers." Their decision-making style is log rolling. Ordinary legislation shares many of the characteristics of constitution writing, but to a lesser degree. The legislators are less synoptic. Ordinary laws are not written for all time but for the foreseeable future. What is done one year can be redone or undone the following year if such proves necessary. Although the annual appropriation procedure is a legislative function it shares many of the incremental features of flow decision making. Policy is formulated in annual units rather than in a single massive *magnum opus*. At the same time there is less self-conscious awareness that the series of budget decisions do add up to an aggregate policy. Still further to the right comes bureaucratic decision making. The decision style is incremental with each case being decided on its individual merits as it arises. The State Depart-

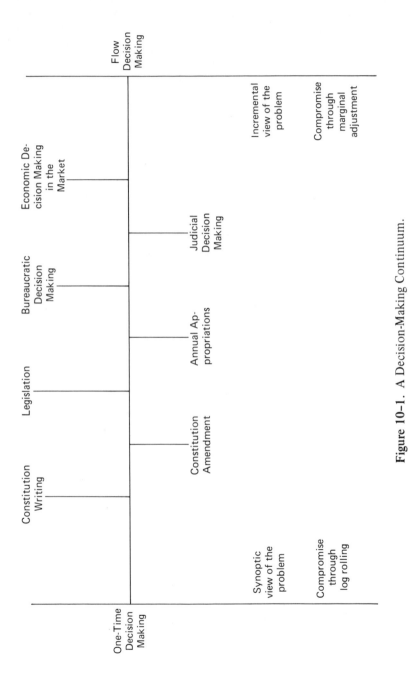

Figure 10-1. A Decision-Making Continuum.

ment, as Andrew Scott has pointed out, is particularly prone to this ad hoc pattern of operation.[9] President Nixon's abolition of the Policy Planning Council reinforced the department's incremental approach by moving synoptic planning out of Foggy Bottom to the White House. The decision-making process of the courts is even more based on flow than that of the bureaucracy. Legal ideology decrees that the courts do not make policy; they only interpret the law on a case by case basis. Only when the aggregate of lower court decisions build up pressure in the form of a dramatic case before the Supreme Court is there much awareness that the courts do formulate policy. Finally, at the extreme right of the continuum may be placed the economic decision making of the market. Through a process of marginal adjustment the various economic actors interact to produce a policy.

This continuum, of course, is only suggestive of one way in which the various types of policy formulation may be categorized. Another dimension is the level of the decision making. That done at a higher level is imposed; that done at a lower level is delegated. Only that done at the same level is considered decision making to the participants. The rest is either rules or trivia depending on whether it comes to be decided above or below.

While this book has generally confined the application of microeconomic theories to the behavior of four departments in the foreign policy arena, these theories of exchange could be applied to other agencies of the bureaucracy. It is reasonable to assume that the Labor Department, NASA, and the Treasury enter into exchange relationships with other departments in the domestic activities that form the bulk of their interest and, indeed, that this represents a general pattern of bureaucratic interaction.

Exchange as a Key to Reform

An exchange theory by its nature is an attack on the normative ideology of hierarchy traditionally held by a bureaucracy. That Weberian view stresses authority relations. The subordinate obeys his superior. In contrast, exchange theory is inherently egalitarian. Each actor is valued for the contribution it can make. The interaction of the various actors works to maximize the total resources. Competition generates efficiency rather than the confusion sometimes projected by the hierarchical ideology. Autonomy is a strength rather than a weakness. An exchange system is flexible rather than rigid.

There is some evidence which suggests that the State Department has stressed hierarchical authority to a greater extent than any other civilian department. The Foreign Service is staffed with a corps of commissioned officers. They are recruited, assigned, and promoted according to a system drawn up along military lines. Abroad diplomatic service resembles military service in many ways. Finally, as von Clausewitz has pointed out, war is an extension of diplomacy, and in reverse, diplomacy is an extension of war. Paul Hammond has observed that after 1871 Western nations recognized the importance of a rapid, coordinated mobilization for war and defense against war.[10] The State Department, as a semi-military bureaucracy, seems to have heeded that lesson, sometimes too well. In some aspects Foggy Bottom seems to be overmobilized. It has insisted on hierarchy when it is not necessarily appropriate. Thus it has become more insistent that its titular jurisdiction over foreign affairs be respected than that certain policies be adopted. It has been more interested in keeping the FSO corps pure than in keeping it effective. In military style the State Department has developed an overabundance of contingency plans. Gordon Tullock decries the tendency of the State Department to become drawn into areas of little consequence. The department develops policies on "such matters as the curriculum for the third grade in Iran, or the location of a glass factory in Korea."[11] Tullock recommends a demobilization. Hierarchy should give way to an "imperial" system in which each provincial governor would have a high degree of autonomy.[12] In the heyday of the British empire the Colonial Office was not particularly eager to communicate with its governors. Each was expected to handle his own problems without recourse to London. The Colonial Secretary confined his attention to appointments and dismissals. At the time telegraph service was extended east of Suez, one Whitehall official is supposed to have asked "Now that we have a cable down to India, do we have anything to say to India?"

Tullock believes that the American diplomatic effort would function more efficiently were it based on an "imperial" system rather than the current disorganized system brought about by an attempt to extend hierarchical control far beyond its practical limits. In its attempt to observe the authority relationships which an analogy to military mobilization demands, the State Department has ensnared itself. Since it is tangled in its own lines of authority to the point of ineffectiveness, it has developed an alternate mode of operation which Tullock calls "bureaucratic free enterprise." Bureaucratic free enterprise is essentially an extension of the model, presented in this book, of various bureaus interacting with each other on the basis of exchange principles. Tullock despairs that "the system of bureaucratic free enterprise has such obvious disadvantages without offsetting advantages that arguments in its favor seem difficult to make."[13] But he does not devote any time to enumerating these "obvious disadvantages." He moves on to suggest reforms which largely amount to decreasing the responsibilities of the State Department to the point where it can handle them on a simplified hierarchical system.[14]

This simplification is a solution to the State Department's problem only if reducing its responsibilities is desired. It will not work if the foreign policy arena and the State Department's role in that arena remains as large as it has been since the Second World War. So long as the arena remains complex, Tullock's simplification has little to offer.

One obvious alternative is to frame reforms in terms of the exchange theories that govern the system of bureaucratic free enterprise. Changing the prices offered for various bureaucratic commodities is one way in which to effect a change in the foreign policy. Higher pay, faster promotions and enhanced status symbols are all ways by which to attract personnel resources into a bureau. An additional vote on an interagency committee will strengthen the bureau which receives it. Raising or lowering the annual appropriations of a bureau is probably the fastest and most direct way to influence its capabilities.

In the bureaucratic market place outcomes will be proportional to the endowments of the agencies participating. A department with extensive resources will have an advantage over one with fewer resources. The State Department appears to have accepted this as a theory of representative bureaucracy. For example, each geographic bureau has a labor advisor whose function it is to represent the labor point of view. The labor attaché fulfills a corresponding role in an embassy abroad. Within the total State Department the Labor Office has the role of spokesman for labor. In formulating general foreign policy this means that the Labor Office speaks for the American working man. In formulating internal administrative policy this means that the Labor Office "looks out" for the labor attachés in personnel matters. In a similar fashion the Economic Bureau and economic advisors represent the economic factors that must be considered in the policy process. Each geographic bureau has some form of regional economic advisor. In turn each country desk has an economic officer. The Economic Bureau represents factors that are world wide in their scope or are too specialized for the geographic bureau economic advisors to stay abreast of, such as finance, aviation, and telecommunications. Science is less well represented. There are no science advisors in the geographic bureaus. This reflects the lesser impact the department views science as having on international relations. At the departmental level the Science Bureau functions to represent science in the same manner as the Labor Office represents the labor viewpoint.

The relative weight given to the different factors—labor, economics, science— in the policy formulation process could be shifted by altering the representation of these factors in the organization of the State Department. More labor specialists, economists or scientists would increase the impact of these considerations in the total policy product. Fewer of these specialists would decrease the impact. A would-be reformer would be well advised to attempt to change the endowments of the various interests as a means of implementing his proposals.

Notes

Notes

Notes to Chapter 1

1. Plato, *The Republic*, Book II in *The Dialogues of Plato*, trans. Benjamin Jowett, vol. I (New York: Random House, 1937), p. 632.

2. Aristotle, *Ethica Nicomachea*, trans. W. D. Ross in *The Works of Aristotle*, vol. IX (London: Oxford University Press, 1915), p. 1132b; H. H. Joachim, *Aristotle: The Nicomachean Ethics*, D. A. Rees, ed. (Oxford: Clarendon Press, 1951), pp. 142-53.

3. Ernest Barker, ed., *Social Contract: Essays by Locke, Hume and Rousseau* (New York: Oxford University Press, Galaxy, 1962), pp. vii-xliv.

4. Georg Simmel, *The Sociology of Georg Simmel*, cited in Peter M. Blau, *Exchange and Power in Social Life* (New York: John Wiley and Sons, 1964), p. 1.

5. George Homans, "Social Behavior as Exchange," *American Journal of Sociology* 63 (1958): 606. See also Homans, *Social Behavior* (New York: Harcourt, Brace and World, 1961).

6. Peter M. Blau, *The Dynamics of Bureaucracy*, 2nd ed. (Chicago: University of Chicago Press, 1963).

7. Kenneth E. Boulding, *Economic Analysis*, 4th ed. (New York: Harper and Row, 1966), hereafter cited as Boulding.

8. Kenneth E. Boulding, *Conflict and Defense* (New York: Harper and Row, Harper Torchbooks, 1963), pp. 16, 19-20, 59, 227.

9. Ralph M. Goldman, "A Transactional Theory of Political Integration and Arms Control," *American Political Science Review* 63 (1969): 721.

10. Talcott Parsons, "On the Concept of Influence," *Public Opinion Quarterly* 27 (1963): 37-62. For a thorough and imaginative critique of Parsons see David A. Baldwin, "Power and Money," *Journal of Politics* 33 (1971): 578-614.

11. James S. Coleman, "Political Money," *American Political Science Review* 64 (1970): 1082-87.

12. Duncan Black, "Lewis Carroll and the Cambridge Mathematical School of P.R.," *Public Choice* 8 (1970): 1-28.

13. James M. Buchanan and Gordon Tullock, *The Calculus of Consent* (Ann Arbor: University of Michigan Press, 1962), p. 63.

14. Mancur Olson, Jr., *The Logic of Collective Action* (New York: Schocken, 1968).

15. Anthony Downs, *An Economic Theory of Democracy* (New York: Harper and Row, 1957).

16. Anthony Downs, *Inside Bureaucracy* (Boston: Little, Brown, 1967).

17. Gordon Tullock, *The Politics of Bureaucracy* (Washington, D.C.: Public Affairs Press, 1965), pp. 102, 105, 200.

18. Charles E. Lindblom, *The Intelligence of Democracy* (New York: The Free Press, 1965).

19. Warren F. Ilchman and Norman Thomas Uphoff, *The Political Economy of Change* (Berkeley and Los Angeles: University of California Press, 1969).

20. Sol Levine and Paul E. White, "Exchange as a Conceptual Framework for the Study of Interorganizational Relationships," *Administrative Science Quarterly* 5 (1961): 583-601.

21. R. L. Curry, Jr., and L. L. Wade, *A Theory of Political Exchange* (Englewood Cliffs, N.J.: Prentice-Hall, 1968); L. L. Wade and R. L. Curry, Jr., *A Logic of Public Policy* (Belmont, Calif.: Wadsworth, 1970).

22. Paul Y. Hammond, "Foreign Policy Making and Administrative Politics," *World Politics* 17 (1965): 656-71.

23. Morton Halperin, Talk before the Department of Political Science General Seminar at Johns Hopkins University, November 12, 1969.

24. Graham T. Allison, "Conceptual Models and the Cuban Missile Crisis," *American Political Science Review* 63 (1969): 689-718, and the expanded version *Essence of Decision: Explaining the Cuban Missile Crisis* (Boston: Little Brown, 1971).

25. Theodore J. Lowi, "American Business, Public Policy, Case Studies, and Political Theory," *World Politics* 16 (1964): 677-715.

26. Robert H. Salisbury, "The Analysis of Public Policy: A Search for Theories and Roles," Chapter 7 in Austin Ranney, ed., *Political Science and Public Policy* (Chicago: Markham, 1968).

27. Lewis A. Froman, Jr., "The Categorization of Policy Contents," Chapter 3 in Ranney, op. cit.

28. Boulding, op. cit., pp. 15-16.

29. Armen A. Alchian and William R. Allen, *Exchange and Production: Theory in Use* (Belmont, Calif.: Wadsworth, 1969), pp. 40-41.

30. Boulding, op. cit., p. 17.

31. Ibid., pp. 20-21.

32. Foreign Assistance Act of 1961, Section 621.

33. Chris Argyris, *Some Causes of Organizational Ineffectiveness Within the Department of State*, Department of State Publication 8180 (January 1967).

34. John Ensor Harr, *The Professional Diplomat* (Princeton: Princeton University Press, 1969), pp. 189-234.

35. Andrew M. Scott, "Environmental Change and Organizational Adaptation," *International Studies Quarterly* 14 (1970): 85-94.

36. David Howard Davis, "The Price of Power," *Public Policy* 18 (1970): 355-82.

37. Cf. John J. Corson and R. Shale Paul, *Men Near the Top* (Baltimore: The Johns Hopkins Press, 1966).

38. Blau, *The Dynamics of Bureaucracy*, pp. 108-113.

39. Erving Goffman, *The Presentation of Self in Everyday Life* (Garden City, N.Y.: Doubleday, Anchor Books, 1959), p. 2.

Notes to Chapter 2

1. Kenneth E. Boulding, *Economic Analysis*, 4th ed., vol. I (New York: Harper and Row, 1966), pp. 19-20.

2. For a general account of this service see Charlton Ogburn, Jr., "The Flow of Policy Making in the Department of State," in Andrew M. Scott and Raymond H. Dawson, *Readings in the Making of American Foreign Policy* (New York: The Macmillan Co., 1965), pp. 284-93.

3. Senate, Committee on Aeronautical and Space Sciences, *NASA Authorization for Fiscal Year 1971: Hearings on S.3374*, 91st Cong., 2nd Sess., March 11, 1970, p. 1053.

4. Senate, Committee on Appropriations, *Departments of Labor and Health, Education and Welfare Appropriations: Hearings on HR 18515 Fiscal Year 1971*, 91st Cong., 2nd Sess., p. 1483.

5. John Ensor Harr, *The Professional Diplomat* (Princeton: Princeton University Press, 1969), pp. 142-45.

6. George L. P. Weaver, "Resources of Other Departments: A Case Study," *The Annals* 380 (1968): 91-92.

7. Department of State, Agency for International Development, Office of Procurement, Participating Agency Staff, "Budget Agreement Between AID and The Department of Labor, Fiscal Year 1970," (unpublished agreement), March 11, 1970.

8. *NASA Authorization for Fiscal Year 1971*, pp. 1060-61.

9. Executive Order 11264, December 31, 1965, 31 F.R. 2; William Barnes and John Heath Morgan, *The Foreign Service of the United States*, Department of State, Bureau of Public Affairs, Historical Office, 1961, p. 257; Robert Ellsworth Elder, *The Policy Machine* (Syracuse: Syracuse University Press, 1960), p. 184.

10. Department of State, *Diplomacy for the 70's*, Publication 8551 (The Macomber Report), December 1970.

11. Treasury, Office of the Secretary, *Annual Report of the National Advisory Council on International Monetary and Financial Policies*, January 30, 1970, pp. 3-4.

12. Senate, Committee on Foreign Relations, *American Institute for Free Labor Development: Hearing*, 91st Cong., 1st Sess., August 1, 1969, p. 58.

13. Jonathan Fuller Galloway, "Space Communications Technology and United States Foreign Policy" (Ph.D. dissertation, Columbia University, 1967), pp. 290-300.

14. Treasury, International Affairs Branch, Office of Industrial Nations, "Recommended Response to Inquiries Regarding Possibility of a Change in the Parity of a Given Currency" (unpublished memorandum), July 10, 1970.

15. House, Committee on Science and Aeronautics, *The Apollo 13 Accident: Hearings*, 91st Cong., 2nd Sess., June 16, 1970, pp. 85, 235, 274; Senate, Committee on Aeronautical and Space Sciences, *Apollo 13 Mission Review: Hearing*, 91st Cong., 2nd Sess., June 30, 1970, pp. 69-72.

16. Harold Nicholson, *Diplomacy*, 3rd ed. (London: Oxford University Press, 1963), p. 44.

17. *NASA Authorization for Fiscal Year 1971*, p. 924.

18. Ibid., p. 1040.

19. Bernard Cohen, *The Political Process and Foreign Policy: The Making of the Japanese Peace Settlement* (Princeton: Princeton University Press, 1957), p. 273.

20. Senate, Committee on Appropriations, *Departments of Labor, and Health, Education, and Welfare Appropriations, Fiscal Year 1970: Hearings on HR 13111*, 91st Cong., 1st Sess., p. 583.

21. *NASA Authorization for Fiscal Year 1971*, pp. 932-34; House, Committee on Foreign Affairs, Subcommittee on National Security Policy and Scientific Developments, *Satellite Broadcasting: Implications for Foreign Policy: Hearings*, 91st Cong., 1st Sess., May 1969, pp. 14-18.

22. Donald R. Mathews, *U.S. Senators and Their World* (Chapel Hill, N.C.: University of North Carolina Press, 1960), pp. 251-54.

23. Francis E. Rourke, *Bureaucracy, Politics and Public Policy* (Boston: Little Brown and Co., 1969), p. 94.

24. Harr, op. cit., p. 141.

25. For an example that candidly reprints the internal "cover letter" memorandum from the State Department to NASA see Senate, Committee on Aeronautical and Space Sciences, *Apollo 13 Mission· Hearing*, 91st Cong., 2nd Sess., April 24, 1970, pp. 31-35. The first, unpublished memorandum from NASA's International Affairs Office to State's Science Bureau on April 28, 1970 requesting that the Science Bureau prepare the testimony closed with this paragraph:

> Grateful for the Department's help on similar occasions in the past weeks, may we turn to you once more?

26. Department of State, "Space Cooperation Agreement between the United States of America and Japan," *Treaties and Other International Acts Series (TIAS)* 6735, July 31, 1969.

27. Department of State, "Treaty on Principles Governing the Activities of States in the Exploration of Outer Space, Including the Moon and other Celestial Bodies," *TIAS* 6347; Senate, Committee on Aeronautical and Space Sciences, *Treaty on . . . Outer Space . . . : Staff Report*, 90th Cong., 1st Sess., March 1967.

28. *TIAS* 6599; Senate, Committee on Aeronautical and Space Sciences, *Agreement on the Rescue of Astronauts, the Return of Astronauts and the Return of Objects Launched Into Outer Space: Staff Report*, 90th Cong., 2nd Sess., July 16, 1968.

29. Bin Cheng, "The 1968 Astronaut Agreement or How Not to Make a Treaty," *Yearbook of World Affairs* 23 (1969): 185-208.

30. Senate, Committee on Finance, *Trade Act of 1970: Hearings*, 91st Cong., 2nd Sess., Oct. 1970, pp. 12-20, 1018-58.

31. House, Committee on Science and Astronautics, Subcommittee on NASA Oversight, *Earth Resources Satellite System: Report*, 90th Cong., 2nd Sess., Dec. 31, 1968.

32. *NASA Authorization for Fiscal Year 1971*, p. 993.

33. *Foreign Policy Implications of Satellite Communications: Hearings*, p. 9; *Satellite Broadcasting: Implications for Foreign Policy: Hearings*, p. 47.

34. Leland B. Yeager, *International Monetary Relations* (New York: Harper and Row, 1966), pp. 189-208.

Notes to Chapter 3

1. Kenneth E. Boulding, *Economic Analysis*, 4th ed., vol. I (New York: Harper and Row, 1966), pp. 22-23.

2. Ibid., pp. 520-23; Armen Alchian, "The Meaning of Utility Measurement" in William Breit and Harold M. Hochman, *Readings in Microeconomics* (New York: Holt, Rinehart and Winston, 1968), pp. 69-88; Paul A. Samuelson, *Economics*, 7th ed. (New York: McGraw-Hill, 1967), pp. 417-25; see also Emil Kauder, *A History of Marginal Utility Theory* (Princeton: Princeton University Press, 1965).

3. Boulding, op. cit., p. 131.

4. For a discussion of a non-substantive agency goal see Mathew Holden, Jr., " 'Imperialism' in Bureaucracy," *American Political Science Review* 60 (1966): 943-51. For an attempt to apply the concept of utility to leadership see Norman Frohlich, Joe A. Oppenheimer, and Oran Young, *Political Leadership and Collective Goods* (Princeton, N.J.: Princeton University Press, 1971).

5. Foreign Assistance Act of 1961, Section 207(e).

6. Jonathan Fuller Galloway, "Space Communications Technology and United States Foreign Policy: 1957-1966" (Ph.D. dissertation, Columbia University, 1967), pp. 365-77.

7. Boulding, op. cit., pp. 22-23.

8. Ibid.

9. National Aeronautics and Space Administration, Office of International Affairs, *NASA International Programs*, p. 30.

10. Ibid.

11. House, Committee on Foreign Affairs, Subcommittee on National Security Policy and Scientific Developments, *Satellite Broadcasting: Implications for Foreign Policy: Hearings*, 91st Cong., 1st Sess., May 1969, pp. 14-16; Senate, Committee on Aeronautical and Space Sciences, *NASA Authorization for Fiscal Year 1969: Hearings*, 90th Cong., 2nd Sess., 1968, p. 124.

12. Senate, Committee on Aeronautical and Space Sciences, *NASA Authorization for Fiscal Year 1971: Hearings on S.3374*, March 11, 1970, pp. 1041, 1061.

13. Ibid., pp. 1041, 1043.

14. Department of Labor, Office of Information, "Shultz Announces Creation of Trade and Adjustment Policy Post at Labor," Press release for AM editions, Monday, January 19, 1970.

15. Armen A. Alchian and William R. Allen, *Exchange and Production: Theory in Use* (Belmont, Calif.: Wadsworth, 1969), pp. 29-32; Boulding, op. cit., pp. 604-08; Kauder, op. cit., pp. 143-45; Samuelson, op. cit., pp. 429-31.

16. *NASA Authorization for Fiscal Year 1971: Hearings*, pp. 397, 575; Senate, Committee on Aeronautical and Space Sciences, *NASA Authorization for Fiscal Year 1969: Hearings on S.2918*, 90th Cong., 2nd Sess., March-April 1968, pp. 609-610.

17. Don E. Kash, *The Politics of Space Cooperation* (Lafayette, Ind.: Purdue University Series, 1967), p. 67.

18. Department of Labor, Bureau of International Labor Affairs, "New Delhi Attaché Conference, *International Labor*, 8:1 (Jan.-Feb. 1967), 2-3; idem., "Tunis Labor Attaché Conference," *International Labor*, 10:3 (July-Aug. 1969), 2-3.

19. R. Duncan Luce and Howard Raiffa, *Games and Decisions* (New York: John Wiley and Sons, 1957), pp. 280-82.

20. L. J. Savage, "The Theory of Statistical Decision," *Journal of the American Statistical Association* 46 (1951): 55-67, cited in Luce and Raiffa, p. 280.

21. Cf. Martin Landau "Redundancy, Rationality and the Problem of Duplication and Overlap," *Public Administration Review* 29 (1969): 346-58.

22. Comsat Corporation, *The Global Satellite System*, January 1970, p. 3.

23. *New York Times*, December 10, 1970.

Notes to Chapter 4

1. Adam Smith, *The Wealth of Nations*, quoted in George J. Stigler, "The Division of Labor Is Limited by the Extent of the Market," in William Breit and Harold M. Hochman,

eds., *Readings in Microeconomics* (New York: Holt, Rinehart and Winston, 1968), p. 152; Kenneth E. Boulding, *Economic Analysis*, 4th ed., vol. I (New York: Harper and Row, 1966), pp. 21, 43.

2. Foreign Assistance Act of 1961 as Amended, Section 621.

3. Cf. André Mathiot, *The British Political System*, Jennifer S. Hines, trans. (Stanford, Calif.: Stanford University Press, 1958), pp. 28, 165-68, 235, 293-301; Anthony Sampson, *Anatomy of Britain Today* (New York: Harper and Row, Harper Colophon Books, 1965), pp. 301-02, 407.

4. Cf. Maurice Duverger, *The French Political System*, Barbara and Robert North, trans. (Chicago: University of Chicago Press, 1958), pp. 45, 47; Henry W. Ehrmann, *Politics in France* (Boston: Little, Brown and Co., 1958), pp. 135, 256-59; Pierre Legendre, *Histoire de L'Administration de 1750 à nos Jours* (Paris: Presses Universitaires de France, 1968), pp. 517-20.

5. National Aeronautics and Space Administration, Office of International Affairs, *NASA International Programs*, January 1970, pp. 16, 23, 30.

6. *Business Week*, January 26, 1952, p. 44. Cited in Joseph R. Fiszman, "The U.S. Labor Attaché," (Ph.D. dissertation, Michigan State University, 1964).

7. William Barnes and John Heath Morgan, *The Foreign Service of the United States*, Department of State, Department and Foreign Service Series 96, pp. 316-17.

8. National Aeronautics and Space Act of 1958, Section 203(b) (6); Communications Satellite Act of 1962, Section 201(b).

9. Burton M. Sapin, *The Making of United States Foreign Policy* (New York: Praeger, 1966), p. 105.

10. John Ensor Harr, *The Professional Diplomat* (Princeton: Princeton University Press, 1969), p. 324; see also testimony of Ellis O. Briggs, Edmund O. Gullion, and others in Senate, Committee on Government Operations, Subcommittee on National Security Staffing and Operations, *Administration of National Security*, 88th Cong., 1965, and the superficial, elitist critique by an insider, John Franklin Campbell, *The Foreign Affairs Fudge Factory* (New York: Basic Books, 1971).

11. Andrew M. Scott, "Environmental Change and Organizational Adaptation: The Problem of the State Department," *International Studies Quarterly* 14 (1970): 85-94.

Notes to Chapter 5

1. Senate, Committee on Government Operations, Subcommittee on National Security Staffing and Operations, *Administration of National Security: Staff Reports and Hearings*, 88th Cong., 1965.

2. Treasury, *Annual Report of the Secretary of the Treasury on the State of the Finances Fiscal Year 1967*, Document No. 3242, 1968, pp. 50-51; idem, *Fiscal Year 1969*, Document No. 3248, 1970, pp. 55, 327-28.

3. Senate, Committee on Finance, *Canadian Automobile Agreement: Hearing*, July 19, 1968.

4. *Annual Report of the Secretary of the Treasury, Fiscal Year 1969*, pp. 50-54, 315-17, 320-25.

5. Joseph R. Fiszman, "The Development of Administrative Roles: The Labor Attaché Program of the U.S. Foreign Service," Chap. 10 in Joseph R. Fiszman, ed., *The American Political Arena* (Boston: Little Brown, 1966).

6. Senate, Committee on Aeronautical and Space Sciences, *NASA Authorization for Fiscal Year 1971: Hearings on S.3374*, 91st Cong., 2nd Sess., pp. 922-23; *The Baltimore Sun*, October 24, 1970; William Hines, "Germans Should Be Wary in Space Deal," *The Washington Star*, February 10, 1970; William J. Normyle, "NASA Offers to Train European Scientists for U.S. Space Missions," *Aviation Week* 84 (February 28, 1966), 23.

7. Armen A. Alchian and William R. Allen, *Exchange and Production: Theory in Use* (Belmont, Calif.: Wadsworth, 1969), pp. 141, 378-89; Kenneth E. Boulding, *Economic Analysis*, 4th ed., vol. I (New York: Harper and Row, 1966), pp. 486-89.

8. Jonathan Fuller Galloway, "Space Communications Technology and United States Foreign Policy," (Ph.D. dissertation, Columbia University, 1967), pp. 572-73.

9. Ibid., pp. 304-78.

10. Ibid., p. 310.

11. *Annual Report of the Secretary of the Treasury, Fiscal Year 1967*, pp. XXV-XXVII, 40, 214-16, 326-27, 368-74.

12. *New York Times*, November 9, December 21 and 30, 1970.

13. Boulding, op. cit., pp. 482-83.

14. Ibid., pp. 483-85.

15. Ibid.

Notes to Chapter 6

1. Executive Order No. 11264, December 31, 1965, 31 F.R. 2; *International Labor*, 11:1 (January-February 1970), 3-4; Department of State, *Diplomacy for the 70's*, Publication 8551, December 1970 (The Macomber Report), pp. 53-92, 261-90.

2. Treasury, Office of the Secretary, *Annual Report of the National Advisory Council on International Monetary and Financial Policies*, 1970, pp. 3-4; Executive Order No. 11269, February 14, 1966, 31 F.R. 2813.

3. Executive Order No. 11075, January 15, 1963; Executive Order No. 11106, April 18, 1963.

4. Senate, Committee on Foreign Relations, *American Institute for Free Labor Development: Hearing*, 91st Cong., 1st Sess., August 1, 1969, pp. 34-37.

5. *International Labor*, 11:1 (January-February 1970), 11.

6. Senate, Committee on Aeronautical and Space Sciences, *NASA Authorization for Fiscal Year 1971: Hearings on S.3374*, 91st Cong., 2nd Sess., March 11, 1970, p. 1040.

7. Department of State, U.S. Information Agency, Office of Policy and Plans, "Report on World Tour of Apollo 12 Astronauts," (unpublished memorandum), April 7, 1970, 1-2.

8. Ibid., p. 4.

9. Ibid., p. 14-2.

10. *Annual Report of the NAC*, 1970, pp. 4, 17.

11. Armen A. Alchian and William R. Allen, *Exchange and Production: Theory in Use* (Belmont, Calif.: Wadsworth, 1969), pp. 54-57; Richard H. Leftwich, *The Price System and Resource Allocation*, 3rd ed. (New York: Holt, Rinehart and Winston, 1966), pp. 66, 75-77.

12. Alchian and Allen, op. cit., p. 56; Leftwich, op. cit., p. 77; Kenneth E. Boulding, *Economic Analysis*, 4th ed. (New York: Harper and Row, 166), vol. I, pp. 627-31.

13. Department of State, Agency for International Development, Office of Procurement, Participating Agency Staff, "Budget Agreement" (sample).

14. Cf. Andrew M. Scott, "Environmental Change and Organizational Adaptation: The Problem of the State Department," *International Studies Quarterly* 14 (1970): 85-94.

15. Senate, Committee on Foreign Relations, *Increased Resources for International Development Association: Hearing on S.3378*, 90th Cong., 2nd Sess., May 21, 1968, p. 6.

16. Gordon Tullock, *The Politics of Bureaucracy* (Washington, D.C.: Public Affairs Press, 1965), pp. 166-67.

Notes to Chapter 7

1. Kenneth E. Boulding, *Economic Analysis*, 4th ed., vol. I (New York: Harper and Row, 1966), pp. 28, 169, 423.

2. Armen A. Alchian and William R. Allen, *Exchange and Production: Theory in Use* (Belmont, Calif.: Wadsworth Publishing Co., 1969), p. 197.

3. Ibid., pp. 63, 153.

4. Ibid.

5. Senate, Committee on Appropriations, *Departments of Labor, and Health, Education and Welfare Appropriations: Hearings on H.R. 18515 Fiscal Year 1971*, 91st Cong., 2nd Sess., p. 1505.

6. National Aeronautics and Space Administration, Office of International Affairs, *NASA International Programs*, Jan. 1970, pp. 1, 2, 5, 6.

7. Senate, Committee on Appropriations, *Departments of Labor, Health, Education and Welfare Appropriations: Hearings on H.R. 18515*, 91st Cong., 2nd Sess., Part 3, pp. 1482-83.

8. John P. Windmuller, "The Foreign Policy Conflict in American Labor," *Political Science Quarterly* 82 (1967): 205-235. *New York Times* (June 4, 5, 9, 10, 11, 14, 17, 23, 1966).

9. Sidney Lens, "Lovestone Diplomacy," *The Nation* (July 5, 1965), p. 14.

10. Serafino Romualdi, *Presidents and Peons* (New York: Funk and Wagnalls, 1967), pp. 15-30.

11. Senate, Committee on Foreign Relations, *American Institute for Free Labor Development: Hearing*, 91st Cong., 1st Sess., August 1, 1969, pp. 1-16; Lens, op. cit., p. 11.

12. Senate, Committee on Foreign Relations, *Foreign Assistance Act, 1969, Hearings on S. 2347*, 91st Cong., 1st Sess., July 14, 15, 18 and August 6, 1969, pp. 72-74; Senate, Committee on Foreign Relations, *American Institute for Free Labor Development*, 91st Cong., 1st Sess., August 1, 1969, pp. 1-10, 68, 84.

13. Department of State, Bureau of International Scientific and Technological Affairs, "Effect of the Apollo 13 Mission on America's Foreign Relations," (May 20, 1970), unpublished memorandum.

14. For typical tracking station agreements see Department of State, "Spain: Tracking Stations Agreement Signed March 11, and 18, 1960," *Treaties and other International Acts Series (TIAS)* 4463; idem., "Union of South Africa: Tracking Stations Agreement Signed Sept. 13, 1960" *(TIAS* 4562).

15. Agricultural Trade Development and Assistance Act of 1954 (PL 480), sec. 103(b).

16. Senate, Committee on Aeronautical and Space Sessions, *NASA Authorization for Fiscal Year 1971, Hearings on S. 3374*, pp. 1043-1044; *New York Times*, August 15 and 16, 1968.

Notes to Chapter 8

1. Senate, Committee on Foreign Relations, *American Institute for Free Labor Development*, 91st Cong., 1st Sess., August 1, 1969, p. 84.

2. Armen A. Alchian and William R. Allen, *Exchange and Production: Theory in Use* (Belmont, Calif.: Wadsworth Publishing Co., 1969), pp. 40-41; Kenneth E. Boulding, *Economic Analysis*, 4th ed., vol. I (New York: Harper and Row, 1966), pp. 33, 50.

3. Department of State, Agency for International Development, Office of Procurement, "Participating Agency Service Agreement" no. VN(LB)3-70 (January 22, 1970); idem., no. LA(LB)50-67, amendment 2 (February 12, 1970); idem., no. FE(LB)2-66, amendment 4 (December 23, 1968), unpublished agreements.

4. Alchian and Allen, op. cit., pp. 125-33.

5. Ibid., p. 126.

6. Department of State, *Diplomacy for the 70's*, Publication 8551 (The Macomber Report), December 1970, p. 270.

7. Boulding, op. cit., 446-53, 501-05.

8. Stephen E. Doyle, "An Analysis of the Socialist States Proposed for Intersputnik: An International Communications Satellite System," *Villanova Law Review* 15 (1969): 83-105.

9. Cf. Alchian and Allen, op. cit., pp. 138-39.

10. Ibid., pp. 44-45.

11. Bureau of the Budget, *The Budget of the United States Government Fiscal Year 1969*, Appendix, p. 709.

12. Boulding, op. cit., pp. 107-08.

13. Senate, Committee on Foreign Relations, *International Development Association: Hearings on HR 33*, 91st Cong., 1st Sess., April 16, 1969, pp. 2-6.

14. For similar instances of the Treasury's realistic knowledge of congressional parsimony see Richard Fenno, *The Power of the Purse* (Boston: Little, Brown, 1966), pp. 372-74.

15. Boulding, op. cit., pp. 86-90, 107-08.

16. Robert Presthus, *The Organizational Society* (New York: Random House, 1962), pp. 164-204.

17. John Ensor Harr, *The Professional Diplomat* (Princeton: Princeton University Press, 1969), pp. 141-42.

18. See Samuel M. Greenhouse, "The Planning-Programming-Budgeting System: Rationale, Language and Idea Relationships," and Francis E. McGilvery, "The Management Accounts Structure," *Public Administration Review*, 26:4 (December 1966).

19. Cf. Aaron Wildavsky, "Rescuing Policy Analysis from PPBS," *Public Administration Review*, 29:2 (March 1969).

20. Burton M. Sapin, *The Making of United States Foreign Policy* (New York: Praeger, 1966), p. 83.

21. Boulding, op. cit., pp. 134-36, 149; Leland B. Yeager, *International Monetary Relations* (New York: Harper and Row, 1966), p. 25.

22. Department of Labor, *Biographic Register of Labor Attachés*, January 1959.

23. Alchian and Allen, op. cit., pp. 181-90; Boulding, op. cit., pp. 136-39; Yeager, op. cit., p. 195.

Notes to Chapter 9

1. Armen A. Alchian and William R. Allen, *Exchange and Production: Theory in Use* (Belmont, Calif.: Wadsworth Publishing Co., 1969), p. 535; Paul A. Samuelson, *Economics*, 7th ed. (New York: McGraw-Hill, 1967), p. 196.

2. Samuelson, op. cit., pp. 411-12.

3. E. Adamson Hoebel, *The Law of Primitive Man* (Cambridge, Mass.: Harvard University Press, 1961), p. 80.

4. Robert L. Peabody, *The Ford-Halleck Minority Leadership Contest, 1965*, Eagleton Institute Cases in Practical Politics, no. 40 (New York: McGraw-Hill, 1966), pp. 34-35.

5. Herbert Kaufman, *The Forest Ranger* (Baltimore: The Johns Hopkins Press, 1967), p. 161.

6. Senate, Committee on Foreign Relations, *American Institute for Free Labor Development: Hearing*, 91st Cong., 1st Sess., August 1, 1969, p. 58; Sidney Lens, "Lovestone Diplomacy," *The Nation*, July 5, 1965, p. 12.

7. Department of Labor, Bureau of International Labor Affairs, "Findings of a Field Trip to North Philadelphia Slums," mimeographed memorandum for the labor packet, July 12, 1967.

8. William Barnes and John Heath Morgan, *The Foreign Service of the United States*, Department of State, Department and Foreign Services Series, No. 96, 1961, pp. 205-09.

9. Laurence F. Schmeckebier, *The Public Health Service*, Service Monographs of the United States Government, No. 10, Institute for Government Research (Baltimore: The Johns Hopkins Press, 1923), pp. 6, 7; Robert Straus, *Medical Care for Seamen* (New Haven: Yale University Press, 1950), p. 41.

10. Department of State, *Diplomacy for the 70's*, Department of State Publication 8551 (The Macomber Report), December 1970, pp. 405-06.

11. Cf. Fritz Machlup, *The Production and Distribution of Knowledge in the United States* (Princeton: Princeton University Press, 1962), p. 114.

12. Samuelson, op. cit., p. 48.

13. *New York Times*, December 14, 1971.

14. Franco Modigliani and Richard Sutch, "Innovations in Interest Rate Policy," *American Economic Review* 56 (1966): 178-96.

15. Leland B. Yeager, *International Monetary Relations* (New York: Harper and Row, 1966), pp. 448, 450, 451.

16. House, Committee on Foreign Affairs, Subcommittee on National Security Policy and Scientific Developments, *Satellite Broadcasting: Implications for Foreign Policy: Hearings*, May 13, 14, 15 and 22, 1969, p. 47.

17. Alchian and Allen, op. cit., pp. 262, 556-57; Samuelson, op. cit., pp. 585-87.

18. Ibid.

19. Jonathan Fuller Galloway, "Space Communications Technology and United States Foreign Policy" (Ph.D. dissertation, Columbia University, 1967), pp. 326-28, 570.

20. David Howard Davis, "The Price of Power," *Public Policy* 18 (1970): 362.

21. *American Institute for Free Labor Development, Hearing*, p. 84; Bernard Nossiter, "Labor and Government Cooperate on Foreign Policy," *The Washington Post*, April 28, 1969, reprinted in Senate, Committee on Foreign Relations, *Foreign Assistance Act, 1969: Hearings on S. 2347*, July 14, 15, and 18 and August 6, 1969, pp. 77-79; Richard Dudman, "Agent Meany," *The New Republic*, May 3, 1969: 13.

22. Cf. *The New York Times*, Washington Bureau, *United States Foreign Policy in the Nixon Administration*, reprinted from the *New York Times*, (January 18-24, 1971): 13-14, 15-17.

Notes to Chapter 10

1. Thorstein Veblen, *The Theory of the Leisure Class* (New York: Macmillan, 1899).

2. Cf. Murray Edelman, *The Symbolic Uses of Politics* (Urbana: University of Illinois Press, 1964), pp. 6-9.

3. Joseph L. Bower, "Descrptive Decision Theory from the 'Administrative' Viewpoint," Chapter 3 in Raymond A. Bauer and Kenneth J. Gergen, *The Study of Policy Foundation* (New York: Free Press, 1968), pp. 141-43.

4. R. Duncan Luce and Howard Raiffa, *Games and Decisions* (New York: John Wiley and Sons, 1957), pp. 275-82.

5. Mancur Olson, *The Logic of Collective Action* (New York: Schocken, 1968).

6. Norman Frohlich and Joe A. Oppenheimer, "I Get By With a Little Help From My Friends," *World Politics* 23 (1970): 104-20.

7. Olson, op. cit., pp. 132-67.

8. Mancur Olson and Richard Zeckhauser, "An Economic Theory of Alliances," *The Review of Economics and Statistics* 48 (1966): 266-79.

9. Andrew M. Scott, "Environmental Change and Organizational Adaptation: The Problem of the State Department," *International Studies Quarterly* 14 (1970): 85-94.

10. Paul Y. Hammond, "Foreign Policy Making and Administrative Politics," *World Politics* 22 (1965): 656-71.

11. Gordon Tullock, *The Politics of Bureaucracy* (Washington, D.C.: Public Affairs Press, 1965), p. 169.

12. Ibid., pp. 170-74.

13. Ibid., pp. 167-70.

14. Ibid., pp. 174-77.

Bibliography

Alchian, Armen A. "The Meaning of Utility Measurement" in William Breit and Harold M. Hochman, eds. *Readings in Microeconomics.* New York: Holt, Rinehart and Winston, 1968.

Alchian, Armen A., and William R. Allen. *Exchange and Production: Theory in Use.* Belmont, Calif.: Wadsworth, 1969.

Allison, Graham T. "Conceptual Models and the Cuban Missile Crisis." *American Political Science Review* 63 (1969): 689-718.

———. *Essence of Decision: Explaining the Cuban Missile Crisis.* Boston: Little Brown, 1971.

Argyris, Chris. *Some Causes of Organizational Ineffectiveness Within the Department of State.* Department of State Publication 8180, January 1967.

Baldwin, David A. "Money and Power." *Journal of Politics* 33 (1971): 578-614.

Barnes, William and John Heath Morgan. *The Foreign Service of the United States.* Department of State, Bureau of Public Affairs, Historical Office, 1961.

Barnett, Vincent M., ed. *The Representation of the United States Abroad.* New York: The American Assembly, Praeger, 1965.

Bauer, Raymond A.; Ithiel de Sola Pool; and Lewis Anthony Dexter. *American Business and Public Policy.* New York: Atherton Press, 1967.

Bauer, Raymond A., and Kenneth J. Gergen. *The Study of Policy Formation.* New York: The Free Press, 1968.

Berger, Henry W. "American Labor Overseas." *The Nation* January 16, 1967.

Black, Duncan. "Lewis Carroll and the Cambridge Mathematical School of P.R." *Public Choice* 8 (1970): 1-28.

Blau, Peter M. *The Dynamics of Bureaucracy,* 2nd ed. Chicago: University of Chicago Press, 1963.

———. *Exchange and Power in Social Life.* New York: John Wiley and Sons, 1964.

Boulding, Kenneth E. *Conflict and Defense.* New York: Harper and Row, Harper Torchbooks, 1963.

———. *Economic Analysis,* 4th ed., vol. I. New York: Harper and Row, 1966.

Buchanan, James M., and Gordon Tullock. *The Calculus of Consent.* Ann Arbor: University of Michigan Press, 1962.

Campbell, John Franklin. *The Foreign Affairs Fudge Factory.* New York: Basic Books, 1971.

Cheng, Bin. "The 1968 Astronaut Agreement or How Not To Make a Treaty." *Yearbook of World Affairs* 23 (1969): 185-208.

Cohen, Bernard C. *The Political Process and Foreign Policy: The Making of the Japanese Peace Settlement.* Princeton: Princeton University Press, 1957.

Coleman, James S. "Political Money." *American Political Science Review* 64 (1970): 1074-87.

Comsat Corporation. *The Global Satellite System.* January 1970.

Corson, John J., and R. Shale Paul. *Men Near the Top.* Baltimore: The Johns Hopkins Press, 1966.

Curry, R.L., Jr., and L.L. Wade. *A Theory of Political Exchange.* Englewood Cliffs, N.J.: Prentice-Hall, 1968.

Davis, David Howard. "The Price of Power." *Public Policy* 18 (1970): 355-82.

Downs, Anthony. *An Economic Theory of Democracy.* New York: Harper and Row, 1957.

———. *Inside Bureaucracy.* Boston: Little, Brown, 1967.

Doyle, Stephen E. "An Analysis of the Socialist States Proposal for Intersputnik: An International Communications Satellite System." *Villanova Law Review* 15 (1969): 83-105.

Dudman, Richard. "Agent Meany." *The New Republic* (May 3, 1969): 13.

Duverger, Maurice. *The French Political System.* Translated by Barbara and Robert North. Chicago: University of Chicago Press, 1958.

Ehrmann, Henry W. *Politics in France.* Boston: Little, Brown, 1958.

Elder, Robert E. *The Foreign Leader Program.* Washington, D.C.: Brookings Institution, 1961.

Elder, Robert E. *The Information Machine.* Syracuse: Syracuse University Press, 1968.
_____. *Overseas Representation and Services for Federal Domestic Agencies.* n.p.: Carnegie Endowment for International Peace, 1965.
_____. *The Policy Machine.* Syracuse: Syracuse University Press, 1960.
Etzioni, Amitai. *The Moondoggle.* Garden City, N.Y.: Doubleday, 1964.
Fenno, Richard F., Jr. *The Power of the Purse.* Boston: Little, Brown, 1966.
Fiszman, Joseph R. "The Development of Administrative Roles: The Labor Attaché Program of the U.S. Foreign Service," Chap. 10 in Joseph R. Fiszman, ed. *The American Political Arena.* Boston: Little, Brown, 1966.
_____. "The U.S. Labor Attaché." Ph.D. dissertation, Michigan State University, 1964.
Frohlich, Norman, and Joe A. Oppenheimer, "I Get By with a Little Help from My Friends." *World Politics* 23 (1970): 104-20.
Frohlich, Norman; Joe A. Oppenheimer; and Oran Young. *Political Leadership and Collective Goods.* Princeton: Princeton University Press, 1971.
Froman, Lewis A., Jr. "The Categorization of Policy Contents," Chapter 3 in Austin Ranney, ed. *Political Science and Public Policy.* Chicago: Markham, 1968.
Griffith, Alison. *The National Aeronautics and Space Act: A Study of the Development of Public Policy.* Washington, D.C.: Public Affairs Press, 1962.
Goffman, Erving. *The Presentation of Self in Everyday Life.* Garden City, N.Y.: Doubleday, Anchor Books, 1959.
Goldman, Ralph M. "A Transactional Theory of Political Integration and Arms Control." *American Political Science Review* 63 (1969): 719-33.
Galloway, Jonathan Fuller. "Space Communications Technology and United States Foreign Policy." Ph.D. dissertation, Columbia University, 1967.
Holden, Mathew, Jr. " 'Imperialism' in Bureaucracy." *American Political Science Review* 60 (1966): 943-51.
Hammond, Paul Y. "Foreign Policy Making and Administrative Politics." *World Politics* 17 (1965): 656-71.
Harr, John Ensor. *The Professional Diplomat.* Princeton: Princeton University Press, 1969.
Homans, George. *Social Behavior.* New York: Harcourt, Brace and World, 1961.
_____. "Social Behavior as Exchange." *American Journal of Sociology* 63 (1958): 597-606.
Ilchman, Warren F., and Norman Uphoff. *The Political Economy of Change.* Berkeley and Los Angeles: University of California Press, 1969.
Kash, Don E. *The Politics of Space Cooperation.* Lafayette, Ind.: Purdue University Series, 1967.
Kauder, Emil. *A History of Marginal Utility Theory.* Princeton: Princeton University Press, 1965.
Kaufman, Herbert. *The Forest Ranger.* Baltimore: The Johns Hopkins Press, 1967.
Kurzman, Don. "Lovestone's Cold War." *The New Republic* (June 25, 1966).
Landau, Martin. "Redundancy, Rationality and the Problem of Duplication and Overlap." *Public Administration Review* 29 (1969): 346-58.
Leftwich, Richard H. *The Price System and Resource Allocation*, 3rd ed. New York: Holt, Rinehart and Winston, 1966.
Legendre, Pierre. *Histoire de L'Administration de 1750 à nos Jours.* Paris: Presses Universitaires de France, 1968.
Lens, Sidney. "Lovestone Diplomacy." *The Nation* (July 5, 1965): 12.
Levine, Sol, and Paul E. White. "Exchange as a Conceptual Framework for the Study of Interorganizational Relationships." *Administrative Science Quarterly* 5 (1961): 583-601.
Lindblom, Charles E. *Bargaining: The Hidden Hand in Government.* RAND-1434, 1955.
_____. *The Intelligence of Democracy.* New York: The Free Press, 1965.
Lodge, George C. *Spearheads of Democracy: Labor in the Developing Countries.* New York: Council on Foreign Relations, Harper and Row, 1962.
Lowi, Theodore J. "American Business, Public Policy, Case Studies, and Political Theory." *World Politics* 16 (1964): 677-715.
Luce, R. Duncan, and Howard Raiffa. *Games and Decisions.* New York: John Wiley and Sons, 1957.
Machlup, Fritz. *The Production and Distribution of Knowledge in the United States.* Princeton: Princeton University Press, 1962.

Mathews, Donald R. *U.S. Senators and Their World.* Chapel Hill, N.C.: University of North Carolina Press, 1960.

Mathiot, André. *The British Political System.* Translated by Jennifer S. Hines. Stanford, Calif.: Stanford University Press, 1958.

Meisler, Stanley. "Meddling in Latin America." *The Nation* (February 10, 1964).

Modigliani, Franco, and Richard Sutch. "Innovations in Interest Rate Policy." *American Economic Review* 56 (1966): 178-96.

New York Times, Washington Bureau. *United States Foreign Policy in the Nixon Administration.* Reprinted from the *New York Times* (January 18-24, 1971).

Nicholson, Harold. *Diplomacy*, 3rd ed. London: Oxford University Press, 1963.

Ogburn, Charlton, Jr. "The Flow of Policy Making in the Department of State," in Andrew M. Scott and Raymond H. Dawson, eds. *Readings in the Making of American Foreign Policy.* New York: The Macmillan Co., 1965.

O'Leary, Michael Kent. *The Politics of American Foreign Aid.* New York: Atherton, 1967.

Olson, Mancur, Jr. *The Logic of Collective Action.* New York: Schocken, 1968.

Paige, Glenn D. *The Korean Decision.* New York: The Free Press, 1968.

Parsons, Talcott. "On the Concept of Influence." *Public Opinion Quarterly* 27 (1963): 37-62.

Peabody, Robert L. *The Ford-Halleck Minority Leadership Contest, 1965.* Eagleton Institute Cases in Practical Politics, no. 40. New York: McGraw-Hill, 1966.

———. *Organizational Authority.* New York: Atherton, 1964.

"Planning, Programming, Budgeting System: A Symposium," *Public Administration Review* 26 (1966): 243-310.

Presthus, Robert. *The Organizational Society.* New York: Random House, 1962.

Ranney, Austin, ed. *Political Science and Public Policy.* Chicago: Markham, 1968.

Ransom, Harry Howe. *Can American Democracy Survive Cold War?* Garden City, N.Y.: Doubleday, Anchor Books, 1964.

Romualdi, Serafino. *Presidents and Peons.* New York: Funk and Wagnalls, 1967.

Rourke, Francis E. *Bureaucracy, Politics and Public Policy.* Little, Brown, 1969.

Salisbury, Robert H. "The Analysis of Public Policy: A Search for Theories and Roles." Chapter 7 in Austin Ranney, ed. *Political Science and Public Policy.* Chicago. Markham, 1968.

Sampson, Anthony. *Anatomy of Britain Today.* New York: Harper and Row, Harper Colophon Books, 1965.

Samuelson, Paul A. *Economics*, 7th ed. New York: McGraw-Hill, 1967.

Sapin, Burton M. *The Making of United States Foreign Policy.* New York: Praeger, 1966.

Scott, Andrew M. "Environmental Change and Organizational Adaptation." *International Studies Quarterly* 14 (1970): 85-94.

Simon, Herbert A. *Administrative Behavior*, 2nd ed. New York: The Free Press, 1965.

Snow, C.P. *Science and Government.* Cambridge: Harvard University Press, 1961.

Stigler, George J. "The Division of Labor is Limited by the Extent of the Market," in William Breit and Harold M. Hochman, eds. *Readings in Microeconomics.* New York: Holt, Rinehart and Winston, 1968.

Thompson, Victor A. *Modern Organization.* New York: Alfred A. Knopf, 1969.

Tullock, Gordon. *The Politics of Bureaucracy.* Washington, D.C.: Public Affairs Press, 1965.

U.S., Department of State. *Diplomacy for the 70's.* Publication 8551 (The Macomber Report), December 1970.

Van Dyke, Vernon. *Pride and Power: The Rationale of the Space Program.* Urbana: University of Illinois, 1964.

Wade, L.L., and R.L. Curry, Jr. *A Logic of Public Policy.* Belmont, Calif.: Wadsworth, 1970.

Weaver, George L.P. "Resources of Other Departments: A Case Study." *The Annals* 380 (1968): 89-96.

Wildavsky, Aaron. "Rescuing Policy Analysis from PPBS." *Public Administration Review* 29:2 (March 1969): 189-202.

———. *The Politics of the Budgetary Process.* Boston: Little, Brown, 1964.

Wilensky, Harold L. *Organizational Intelligence.* New York: Basic Books, 1967.

Windmuller, John P. "The Foreign Policy Conflict in American Labor." *Political Science Quarterly* 82 (1967): 205-35.

———. "Labor: A Partner in American Foreign Policy?" *The Annals* 350 (1963): 104-114.

Yeager, Leland B. *International Monetary Relations.* New York: Harper and Row, 1966.

Index

About the Author

David Howard Davis is a native of Washington, D.C., as befits a student of the federal bureaucracy. He was educated at the International School of Geneva and at Cornell University, where in 1963 he received his A.B. in government. He served three years in the army as an artillery officer, first in Korea then in Vietnam. In 1967, he began his graduate studies in political science at The Johns Hopkins University. In 1969 he received his M.A. degree for an essay on post-revolutionary politics in Algeria. The following year The Woodrow Wilson Foundation awarded Mr. Davis a fellowship to study the State Department's relations with domestic departments operating in the foreign policy arena. This study for which The Johns Hopkins University granted the author a Ph.D. in 1971, is the basis of the present book.

The author is currently on the political science faculty of Rutgers University, where he teaches courses on foreign policy and organizational theory.

B6.